WHITE FRAGILITY AND RACISM

Impacts of cynical mindset on racism in America.

Anti-Racism, Discrimination, privilege, rage, and white supremacy

© **Courtney Fernandez**

Table of Contents

INTRODUCTION — 4

CHAPTER 1: CONCEPT AND FACTS ABOUT RACISM — 7

CHAPTER 2: RACISM, CHILDREN AND EDUCATION — 17
- Forestalling racism in schools — 21

CHAPTER 3: CAUSES AND EFFECTS OF RACISM — 26
- The Main Causes of Racism — 26
- Causes of racism in children — 30
- The Effects of Racism — 31

CHAPTER 4: ANTI-RACISM — 34
- How to Become Anti-Racist as a White Person — 35
- Responsibilities of a White Anti-Racist — 37
- How to be Anti-Racist as a Person of Color — 39
- Different Ways To Be Antiracist — 41
  - 1) Understand the meaning of racist. — 41
  - 2) Stop saying, "I'm not racist." — 42
  - 3) Identify racial imbalances and differences. — 43
  - 4) Confront the racist thoughts you've held or kept on holding. — 44
  - 5) Understand how your antiracism should be intersectional. — 45
  - 6) Champion antiracist thoughts and strategies. — 45
- Responsibilities of a Colored Anti-Racist — 46

CHAPTER 5: COMBATING RACISM AND XENOPHOBIA — 49

CHAPTER 6: CONCEPT THAT YOU SHOULD KNOW AND TEACH YOUR CHILDREN — 57

CHAPTER 7: MISTAKES PARENTS/GUARDIAN MAKE WHILE EDUCATING KIDS — 79

CHAPTER 8: DISCRIMINATION — 85
- Racial Zoning and Ghetto — 96
- Ghettos And Crime — 97
- Crime Is A Ghetto Career — 100
- Ghetto Attitudes Towards Crime — 102
- Black Racism In The Media — 103

CHAPTER 9: HOW TO END RACISM?	**106**
Uprooting racism	110
CHAPTER 10: THE IMPORTANCE OF ACHIEVING YOUR DREAMS	**128**
Facts about Confident People	131
CONCLUSION	**133**

Introduction

Are you looking forward to easy, crystal clear, and straightforward answers to questions about racism? About where it originated and why it is still alive after all this time? You might be slightly disappointed because these are very broad, complex, and controversial issues.

Racism isn't the easiest term to define, and as you read on, you will understand why. Brief and compact definitions can sometimes be misleading, although, in certain situations, these tight definitions are unavoidable. This book is a good example of such situations. Understanding and fighting racism requires you to know and have all the pieces on the board, pieces that I have simplified and brought to you in this book.

Taking a look at the system of racism, even from a distance, will reveal the unearned privileges and advantages being granted to white or light-skinned people simply because of their race. White people are constantly faced with their societal values, unlike people of color. One gets to see their histories in approved school textbooks, positive portrayals by the media, advantages of quality education, great healthcare, safe neighborhoods, high-paying jobs, and so on. The other is often deprived of quality education and healthcare, high-paying jobs, proper legal aid, and so on. By now, you must know which race gets what, and this kind of bias is unfair. All this is due to being raised in a society that is drenched in racism. Eventually, everyone has to absorb implicit and explicit stereotyped knowledge from the community, schools, and even families concerning the value of white folks and people of color. This results in people learning racial stereotyping, acting on those stereotypes consciously or unconsciously, without giving themselves time to rethink or criticize those beliefs. These beliefs have created and still create wounds of loss, pain, and grief for those who happen to fall below the white line.

When you have functioned and still function based on internalized stereotypes of people and their races, understanding just how much you are being influenced by white supremacy becomes difficult. People of color have been faced with limited opportunities, marginalized identities, and barriers for centuries. At the same time, white folks find themselves prospering in a society that grants them privileges whether they deserve it or not. There are not enough conversations about it besides posts on social media and town hall meetings now and then. This is just one reason why it is so difficult to understand the true meaning of racism, how to identify, and how it should be handled. People are increasingly becoming able to identify racism, but the problem of handling it remains. How you interrupt or respond to a racist comment or joke is a vital tool in erasing this disease in our time, and this book is a comprehensive guide to do just that.

Chapter 1: Concept and facts about racism

This was not important a few decades ago. Child racism was a natural precursor to growing up in a racist class society, in which the majority sought to preserve their racial, religious, and class gains by preventing minority or disagreements from leaking to positions or places that might make them appear equals or equal.

This was very easy. Even the governments used to cover the racist tendency of the gentlemen's class through the laws of apartheid between whites and blacks, between citizens and foreigners, between the rich and the poor, and between different religions. This separation started with civil rights such as election, candidacy, and even work in public areas or high professions. , And it does not end in the separation of students in schools, between passengers in buses, between markets, bars, and even homes.

With the collapse of the extreme right in Germany after the Second World War, the Europeans regained their calculations of the effectiveness of its racism and its hopes with shame, then the uprising of the Africans in America came to draw new features to reject and reject racism, and perhaps we all owe it to Rosa Parks, who sparked the uprising that provided the opportunity to fight racism worldwide.

If whites inherited a long history of practicing racism, while blacks inherited a long history of being subjected to persecution, this does not mean that the practice of racism or submission has a fixed innate advantage to a color or a specific race, but rather this perception by itself is a shameless embodiment of racism.

THE PERCEPTION OF RACE

In later years, various indices could be used to describe health status. Such indices include mortality (e.g., all causes, life expectancy, heart disease, malignant neoplasms, and cerebrovascular disease), medical diseases (e.g., hypertension and cancer), and subjective health status. Many of the major racial (Asian, Black, Pacific Islander, Native American, and white) and ethnic (Hispanic) groups in the U.S., previously referred to as ethnic groups, differ concerning these health indices.

PERCEIVED RACISM

Racism as a stress source

An emerging body of research shows that racism (whether perceived or not) is a potential source of acute and chronic stress for many members of ethnic groups, including Caucasians. Individual and institutional racism as an additional source of stress can contribute through distal and proximal pathways to the interethnic group disparities in health. Distal mechanisms involve internal and external factors that are hypothesized to mediate the relationship between environmental events and interpretations of events. These include involving bias and involving injury, danger, or challenge. Importantly, the subjective aspect of perceived racism a priori precludes deciding stress (i.e., perception of harm, threat, or challenge). On the other hand, proximal pathways are postulated to more directly influence psychological (e.g., anger) and physiological (e.g., sympathetic nervous system and immune activity) stress reactions or tertiary outcomes (e.g., cardiovascular disease, depression, low birth weight, and cancer).

Building on existing conceptualizations, the underlying premise of this proposed model is that sociodemographic factors, constitutional factors, and coping resources mitigate the perception of an environmental stimulus as involving racism and involving harm, threat, or challenge. Once the stimulus is perceived to be involving racism and harm, a threat or challenge will result in psychological and physiological stress reactions followed by coping responses. Over time, these psychological and physiological systems are activated and adapted repeatedly to lead to an allostatic burden that, in turn, increases the risk of adverse health outcomes.

To the degree that

(1) Perceived racism evokes the psychological and physiological reactions people experience, and

(2) The unequal allostatic strain associated with perceived racism is found along ethnic-gender lines, this model may provide a more context-specific basis for understanding the association between perceived racism and health inequalities in later years. While perceptions of discrimination associated with other "isms" (e.g., ageism, classism, and sexism) as well as perceptions of other stressors (e.g., cultural stress) are likely to be similarly related to This chapter would be devoted to the social and physiological workings of the topic of ethnically related injustices and disparities., psychological and physiological functioning.

Answers to psychological and physiological questions

To obey definitions of prejudice (e.g., psychological and physiological) are presented multiple responses from different systems. The psychological reactions include anger, helplessness, desperation, anxiety, resentment, fear, and cardiovascular, immune, and neuroendocrine systems involved in the physiological responses. Although cardiac contraction, vasodilatation, vasoconstriction, vasoconstriction, and reduced-sodium excretion are among the cardiovascular responses, Immune response to chronic stress entails most commonly cellular and humoral responses, which requires lower natural-killer cell activation which repression of B- and T-lymphocytes that improve vulnerability to disease.

Coping with Answers

Coping with responses and behaviors (coping with responses) requires attempts made by or tools made available to individuals to handle intrinsic and extrinsic stimuli viewed as stressful. Though there are numerous coping conceptualizations (e.g., approach, avoidance, emotion-focused, problem-focused, and cognitive), these strategies can be either active or passive. More active responses involve efforts to alter the nature of the interaction between the person and the environment (e.g., problem-solving). More passive responses, by contrast, include efforts to manage "distress" that results from the perceived stressor (e.g., self-medication). It remains to be determined whether individuals use similar responses to coping with managing stressors, or whether coping responses rely on context.

To the degree that coping strategies partly mitigate individual variations in psychological and physiological responses to perceived bias, these strategies are expected to affect late adult allostatic loads. Because of the positive consequences associated with their coping strategies and identification types, members of ethnic minority communities who progress to late adulthood have undoubtedly done so in the light of life stories rife with persistent vulnerability to prejudice. In one probability survey of black people, for example, LaVeist, Sellars, and Neighbors (2001) found that individuals who are subject to bigotry relate those adverse interactions to cultural and social activities to personal deficiencies — were more likely to survive the 13-year follow-up period.

Relatively few studies have looked at the relationships between perceived bias, coping, and state of health. The directions of the relationships were dependent on the outcome of the studies which were conducted. For example, in a sample of females from black college, some passive and active responses to coping with blood pressure and heart rate responses were positively related. Both approaches came back to cardiovascular responses, as well.

Williams et al. (1997a) also observed that passive and aggressive reactions to unequal treatment (including ethnic group discrimination) were significantly associated with psychological pain, reduced well-being and health illnesses among blacks and whites in a chance survey of black and white individuals. In another study exploring the consequences of dealing with unequal care and raising blood pressure.

Krieger and Sidney (1996) found that higher rates of resting blood pressure were correlated with more proactive approaches in the black working class. Symptoms of depression were higher in Asian refugees high in perceived discrimination and high in the use of passive coping strategies compared to those lower in perceived discrimination and low in the use of passive coping.

Allostasis involves the attainment or maintenance by the change of physiological systems. Though not mentioned in this way, allostasis may initially be viewed as the physiological counterpart of coping. If Mr. Leach, for example, was a lower SES black male with a dark skin tone in his mid-60s, came to respond to fairly chronic perceptions of interethnic community and inter-ethnic racism by momentarily withdrawing himself from the world to "collect himself and regroup." a coping response that leads to the blunting and removal of aggressive feelings, and a marked decrease in heart rate, he would have While probably beneficial in the short term (e.g., measurable reduction in psychological and physiological responses), persistent attempts to sustain psychological and physiological processes may have associated costs in response to recurrent perceptions of racism." Everything is equal (e.g., age, socioeconomic resources, occupational status, and educational achievement), compare to Mr. Leach 's psychological axis. The same amount of racism from interethnic groups but did not perceive prejudice from interethnic groups because its skin tone is slightly lighter than a brown bag of paper.

Corporate racism

Even if there is no perception of prejudice, systemic forms of racism can directly affect health through limited access to health care or high-quality health care. For example, research indicates that ethnic minorities (usual blacks) are less likely to obtain selected cardiovascular procedures and renal procedures than whites, despite some zero findings. Regarding their older French-Canadian, English-Canadian, and Portuguese counterparts, institutional racism has contributed to limited or blocked social and health services for Montreal's Chinese elders. Similarly, older Mexican Americans have observed the contribution of institutional practices to problems with health access. Research shows that those ethnic groups are biased:

- Begin at medical school.
- Are observed among black and white doctors.
- Are present before adulthood in the treatment of the patient population.

Allostatic effects on load and safety

The accumulated negative effects associated with psychological and physiological system maintenance are referred to as the allostatic charge. The stress response systems involved (e.g., psychological, immune, cardiovascular, and neuroendocrine) are the same as those posed to contribute to allostatic loads. This burden is postulated to increase the risk of adverse health outcomes. Essentially, these systems are not acting in isolation. Instead, they are often complexly interrelated.

Psychological sequelae include cognitive declines and persistent alterations to the mood state. To the degree that acute perceptions of racism are associated with enhanced neuroendocrine responses and stimulating neurotransmitter amino acid production resulting in decreased hippocampal volume, chronic perceptions of racism may be correlated with cognitive impairment for those who are disproportionately exposed in later years. Although the literature is mixed on disparities in mental health, research suggests that perceptions of racism relate positively to mood deficits. Ethnic differences in depression prevalence in later years could develop secondary to the untoward effects of perceived racism through chronic feelings of uncontrollability, helplessness, and self-esteem threats.

Hypertension, stroke, and heart disease comprise cardiovascular and cerebrovascular outcomes. If racism perceptions are related to acute elevations in vascular reactivity, leading to hyperactivity, structural changes in the vasculature, and alterations in the baroreceptor, it is plausible that chronic perceptions of racism could contribute to the eventual development of hypertension in later years.

While no published research could be found that directly explored the relationship between perceived racism and immune results, there is no reason to conclude that as a stressor, specific humoral and cellular responses are correlated with chronic perceptions of racism. The one caveat is that unlike other recurrent stressors that people may get used to, the degree to which people are accustomed to perceptions of racism is not understood.

Chapter 2: Racism, children and education

Racism is consistently a troublesome theme however the news and online platforms give proof that it despite everything exists and keeps on affecting how we draw in with one another in the United States. Racism is scholarly conduct where we are associated to see contrast and follow up on it. Racism is common to the point that it causes difficulties for learning and with school encounters.

Racial inclination in our schools influences understudy learning and school discipline, just as impacts how understudies connect. Negative racial perspectives and practices are imbued in our framework and foundations. Be that as it may, as teachers we have the chance to change results in our schools disregarding our current frameworks.

The initial step to understanding racism is recognizing that it is woven into American history. It began well before now, yet we are as yet encountering a wave of negative impacts.

Racism is the demonstration of oppression an alternate race dependent on the conviction or presumption that one's race is unrivaled. The unintended practices and results of racism are inescapable to such an extent that it is now and again hard to recognize how it influences us. One way is a racial predisposition, which tends to the perspectives or generalizations that influence our activities toward a gathering of individuals unknowingly.

Here are three territories where the circumstances and logical results of racism is evident in schools

School Discipline

Cause: Racial inclination in school pioneers and educators influences how they draw in with understudies. Learned negative generalizations direct how we connect with various racial gatherings. For understudies, this can affect how an instructor sees their learning capacity, commitment in school exercises and how they may decipher understudy conduct decisions.

Impact: According to the US Government Accountability Office Report on Discipline Disparities, dark understudies have excessively suspended in schools the nation over. These equivalent understudies are bound to be truant or become transient understudies inside the locale. If an instructor accepts negative generalizations about an understudy, at that point they are bound to rebuff them for little peaceful offenses. As school disciplinary activity expands, understudies miss expanding measures of guidance.

School Funding

Cause: School subsidizing and assets are connected to state and nearby assets. There are occurrences where understudies from low-salary or under-resourced schools are deciding to take a crack at specific well-resourced schools. The absence of school assets is a sign of how racially one-sided strategies underserve certain networks. This occurs through lodging approaches that advise school zoning and have prompted a reaction of actualizing magnet programs or transporting arrangements.

Impact: The absence of adequate assets and underfunding straightforwardly impacts scholastic accomplishment. Generally, dark and earthy colored understudies who have gone to ineffectively financed schools additionally have had lacking learning openings. This adds to the accomplishment hole which features the huge contrasts in scholarly execution across racial lines. It is clear that long periods of being underserved in below-average conditions impact results. On the off chance that we finance schools unjustly, at that point we keep on sustaining the racially one-sided lodging and subsidizing strategies that caused the underlying asset issue.

School Security

Cause: Negative generalizations about dark and earthy colored understudies are exacerbated through the media. There are regularly pictures and clasps that depict these youngsters as rough or forceful. For instance, I read an article of white understudies busting windows of vehicles, lighting fires, and destroying a school grounds after a university b-ball match dominate, and it was portrayed as a "festival". A comparable picture appeared with a gathering of dark understudies fighting ground strategies with signs, remaining on vehicles and that was portrayed as a "revolt". The photograph with black understudies incorporated a subtitle that raised wellbeing worries for the overall population and urged school grounds to build security and disciplinary activity, where the photograph of white understudies didn't. This story just fortifies the negative generalization of dark and earthy colored youth as compromising or hazardous individuals from our locale.

Impact: Whether school authority knows about it or not, these pictures are subliminally advising how choices are made. For this situation, there are school pioneers who foundation safety efforts in their schools under the idea that they are expanding security. The inquiry is, who is it they accept to be dangerous? This sends a negative message to understudies about what their identity is and how they are seen while additionally propagating a cultural message that they are dreaded.

Forestalling racism in schools

Awareness

The first means of forestalling racism in quite a while is mindfulness and self-reflection.

Teachers must perceive how the convergences of race, ethnicity, sex, sexual direction, religion, financial status, and being capable affect us separately. We should see how our recognizable proof inside a specific gathering gives us benefit in specific spaces and we should be available to effectively tune in to underestimated bunches who experience life diversely due to their social groupings. We should recognize our predispositions and look to comprehend individuals with various encounters.

Proficient Development

Notwithstanding mindfulness, instructors must put resources into proficient improvement openings that expand their social skills. During the school year search for proficient learning openings that emphasize socially applicable education, social fitness, decent variety, and multiculturalism. Use assets, for example, Rethinking Schools and Teaching Tolerance, which center on decent variety and value in instruction.

Additionally look at our past post, How Teachers in Diverse Schools Can Improve Their Cultural Competence.

Socially Relevant Teaching

Educators can make learning openings that recognize race and ethnicity, and organize forestalling racism through social equity with socially significant instructing. Socially applicable educating underlines scholarly greatness, social ability, and social and political examination. Through socially important educating, understudies are occupied with thorough learning encounters that utilization text and assets to investigate issues inside differing networks. Moreover, there is an accentuation on social equity and social activism.

Socially important showing utilizes different writings to address troublesome issues of race, culture, and ethnicity in astute ways. The content may enhance general reading material to give verifiable data that isn't standard.

Socially important showing opens understudies to an assortment of individuals and conditions. It is about the profundity of information and goes a long way past a social gathering where understudies taste nourishments and hear music from another culture. Above all, socially applicable instructing advances social equity and features chronicled developments that have attempted to advance resistance and value far and wide.

Unequivocal Lessons on Race and Conflict Resolution

To forestall racism instructors must converse with understudies expressly about racism.

Conversations about race can be awkward, yet with appropriate arranging, undivided attention, and an acknowledgment of everybody's shared weakness, and at first awkward discussion can turn into a transformative learning experience. At the point when we find out about societies yet don't discuss the troublesome parts of our history, we do an insult to our understudies and our general public.

We should set aside an effort to talk about social false impressions and the battles our nation has confronted while tending to racism. Both of these assets talk about national and worldwide recent developments during a time proper way.

Books are likewise a fantastic method to talk about troublesome subjects of race, diversity, and multiculturalism.

Familiarity with How Racial Bias

Impacts Discipline

As indicated by the U.S. Training

Department's Civil Rights Data Collection, Black understudies are suspended or removed at multiple times the pace of their white friends. Also, in 2011-2012, Black young ladies were suspended at a pace of 12%, a lot more noteworthy than young ladies of different ethnicities and most classes of young men.

Racism influences how Black and Brown's understudies are taught all through schools in the United States. Schools must know about the racial predisposition that can influence how understudies are trained. Pioneers and instructors must utilize information to investigate inclines in understudy conduct and reveal disproportionality. Schools can likewise execute Restorative Practices to give a helpful, as opposed to a correctional, way to deal with school discipline.

Network Partnerships

The impacts of racism are foundational and extensive. When understudies have found out about racism they should go out into the world and interface with these issues continuously.

Schools must band together with network associations who are battling issues of racism and value in their locale.

Social equity is a sign of part of forestalling racism. Welcoming people group associations into schools is a magnificent method to get understudies engaged with social equity work. Also, welcoming families into your homeroom to discuss their way of life or encounters that line up with a specific point is a decent method to make network and show your understudies that their encounters and the encounters of their families are similarly as significant as the accounts they read about in books.

The 1964 Civil Rights Act ensured equivalent access to instruction, anyway over 50 years after the fact the impacts of racism have made instructive open door holes that hugely affect understudies of shading in the United States.

We should be purposeful about forestalling racism in our schools.

Chapter 3: Causes and Effects of Racism

If we're going to effectively tackle the problem of racism and eventually uproot it from our way of living and thinking, then it is important to dive into the causes of racism. When we can identify the cause, we can find ways to make the real changes that are desperately needed.

The Main Causes of Racism

1. An Instinctive Feeling of Responsibility to Protect One's Social Race. It is instinctive to feel connected to anyone with whom we feel similar. It's normal to feel a certain level 0f comfort when we are among people who reflect us in behavior and appearance. Humans are easily triggered by anything that threatens to put anything we care about, from our territory to family to identity and culture, in harm's way. Racism is the extreme and misdirected form of human nature to protect anything we deem valuable. So, if something or someone doesn't seem to fit into the same group, they are quickly perceived as a threat, inferior, or both.

2. Fear of Displacement and Loss. Humans are instinctive protectors of their people and position, which means that they fear any loss of either or both of those things. It ranges from social status to possessions, territory, and even jobs. Humans are naturally afraid of being displaced by anyone who seems better and more appealing than they are. When you are replaced by someone better than you, you feel unworthy, don't you? This is not an attempt to justify racism, but fear is one of its biggest and worst sponsors. Nobody wants to lose anything. Not people, not a territory, and not their rights.

3. Ignorance. This is the product of being unaware, uninformed, or uneducated, and this drives racism even in the 21st century. Being raised a certain way all your life, and watching everyone around you function the same way can fool you into believing a thing to be right despite it being morally wrong. Having another human being who doesn't share the same sentiments as you can make you feel a little uneasy sometimes. So many people don't see their actions, thoughts, and words as racist, because they genuinely believe they are correct. Putting an end to this ignorance can only be done by creating awareness, educating people on the errors of their ways, as well as the consequences that follow. Until ignorance is uprooted by proper education, racism will continue to eat deep into the hearts of humans.

4. *A Lack of Self-Love and the Desire to Feel Worthy and Superior*. The most racist of the bunch tend to be the ones without self-confidence, any kind of esteem, and — chief of all — self-love. A racist persona projects all that negative energy onto people that are considered vulnerable, inferior, and weak. You can only truly appreciate another person if you truly love and appreciate everything that you are. Racism is rooted in feelings of worthlessness, envy, and feelings of victimization. Some people tend to take out their failures on other people, and racists are no different. Racists are usually filled with feelings of insignificance, isolation, being unloved, and offended, leading them to put all that energy into blaming and hating another person. Racism is an individual act that can only be fixed by confronting these individual feelings and actions.

5. *Having a Pro-Racist Family Background*. Parents have more impact on their children's thoughts and beliefs than they might realize. Children note down their parent's reactions to a person from another race and work to emulate it without even feeling the need to know why. If a white parent treats an Asian American harshly in front of their child, the child simply assumes that it was the right course of action. After all, "Mommy did it." Hate is born in the family and can be hard to correct. Upbringing plays an important role in your personality and values.

6. *Pressure from Friends*. People are easily influenced by peer pressure more than they realize, and even as significantly as they are influenced by their parents. You are more likely to listen to the

people you have chosen as your friends, which mea
you are also more inclined to agree with things they
say — and that includes views on people of color.
This is a major cause of racism.

7. Personal Experiences. If you have ever
experienced any form of assault from a member of a
certain race, there's a high chance that you end up
living in fear of the entire race. It is completely
normal for people to feel this way. It is what happens
after you get heartbroken or betrayed by someone you
cared about. There's a good chance you develop a
strong opinion against that person's culture, and not a
good one. This fear, this survival instinct, can
manifest as racism and impair your judgment.

8. Stereotypes. This is a major cause of racism. It is
conveyed through radio, music, television, books, and,
most importantly, the internet. Stereotyping believes
all members of a group think and act the same way
because of how a member behaves or is portrayed.
Whenever an impressionable person is introduced to
stereotypes or people who have been stereotyped, they
quickly conclude that other people in that category
must act and think alike. People of color have been
stereotyped all over the world, and the younger
generation is picking up on these cues.

9. Unfamiliarity. This is another common cause of
racial bias. Some people who live in fear of the

unknown. Anything they don't know or understand is a source of fear for them, and that includes people of other cultures. A child who is raised and surrounded by only people from their race has the possibility of becoming racist. That possibility increases when they have been fed with negative stereotypes about other races. This isn't necessarily what happens every time, but when combined with stereotyping and a lack of experience with other races, it slowly builds into a racist mentality. For this reason, children must be taught and be allowed to experience diversity so that their minds can absorb the right information and build a solid anti-racist foundation in preparation for the future.

Causes of racism in children

One of the causes of racism that parents convey to their children is the desire to protect them, protecting them from mixing with other races or cultures that threaten the system that parents are trying to preserve, this fear of the child acquiring different convictions pushes parents to place the child in a closed circle of the children of the same race, then from the children of Religion itself, then from the people of the city, the neighborhood and the neighborhood, and narrowing the circle until the child finds himself barely accepting someone who speaks in a different accent or wears his shirt differently.

Unfortunately, if this protection was effective in the past to promote social satisfaction that depends on belonging to a class, then it is in the modern world that it gives the opposite effect. The results of racism on the social level mean less ability to integrate into school and different activities, then less ability to Finding the right job and achieving integration in the work environment. Also, the racist in the modern era is considered a pariah.

On the other hand, people who are subjected to racism suffer from health and psychological problems that seem to be closely related to the experience of racism, as research indicates, such as anxiety, depression, premature aging, and even obesity diseases.

The Effects of Racism

First, let's address the effects of racism on society. A society powered by a racist mentality restricts some citizens from participating and contributing to the collective progress of the nation, and this puts a damper on development and success. If a good amount of a society's population does not have access to the same privileges as the others, they will always be a few steps behind. Victims of racism tend to lack employment and academic opportunities that would have given them the chance to give back to society, ensuring the overall wellbeing of the country's economy.

Another thing to note is that discriminating against an entire race limits them from fully being a part of the country's culture. This causes other citizens to not fully appreciate the differences and similarities among them, which results in social inactivity and the continuation of racism in the future.

Living comfortably with racism keeps the country at a disadvantage because the result will be aggression, cruelty, and sheer violence on a national or local scale. If bad blood is allowed to accumulate between groups in the community, it's a one-way street to isolated incidents, verbal and physical confrontations, and other forms of low-level negativity. Racial intolerance and discrimination are a recipe for riots, fights, and even war.

Racism also has effects on an individual level. Individuals who are faced with racial bias every day find that their lives become very restricted. Fear becomes an all too familiar feeling, with low self-esteem as a regular side effect. When a person experiences persecution and discrimination every day of their life, they eventually they conclude that they are as unworthy as people say, and this only works in favor of the oppressors.

Anyone who attributes little value to themselves rarely makes an effort to achieve more than they already have, and this leads to family generation drenched in disadvantages. Also, it is common for victims of racism to grow into resentful, defensive, and aggressive individuals who look to criminal activity as a way to rebel against injustice. However, this just serves to keep them at a disadvantage.

Another tragic effect of racism is death through hate crimes and police brutality, which often appears to have no consequences. Countless people have died because society saw their lives as inferior and insignificant, and these deaths affect more than just the person who died. That person was a parent, a spouse, an uncle or aunt, a friend, a colleague, and so on. Imagine being murdered just for having the "wrong" skin color.

Chapter 4: Anti-Racism

Do you know what it means to be anti-racist? An anti-racist isn't simply a person who doesn't hate people of color. The term is used to refer to people who are actively raising their consciousness about racial bias and taking action when they experience an act of racism.

An anti-racist is very different from a nonracist. A nonracist has beliefs against racial inequality and white privilege, but when it comes to overt acts of racism like police brutality, hate crimes, and murder, they would rather watch it on the news or Instagram and just do nothing about it.

Identifying with anti-racism means that you are actively cultivating a new moral code, one that is a combination of commitment against racism, and action to fight against and end the racist actions committed every day against people who did nothing to deserve it all.

It is not enough to say that you are not racist. A verbal proclamation isn't enough to heal from the disease. You have to be intentional and active about it. You need to acknowledge that racism is your problem as well as everyone else's, and you need to be determined to take action against it. However, being anti-racist as a white person has different requirements than it does for a person of color. So we will be taking a look at what it means to be anti-racist for both parties.

How to Become Anti-Racist as a White Person

Becoming an anti-racist as a white person is a journey you embark on while you are still evolving and discovering your own racial identity. For example, once you are done being oblivious about your privileges as a white person, the next step is integrative awareness, where you discover the significance of your skin color and how you can use that to your advantage.

The ways you use your white privilege to alter your internalized feelings about race and take action when you see an act of racial partiality are a huge part of your anti-racist identity development. Tema Okun wrote about anti-racism in her article titled White Supremacy Culture. She made referred to her journey to anti-racism as a white person, and I would like to share her list of ways to achieve this:

1. You have to see yourself as a member of "the White group."

2. You must begin to understand and be responsible for the power you are entitled to as a member of the white group. This entails acknowledging the history of white supremacy and understanding that the privilege

you enjoy as a result of the mistakes your ancestors made is very real.

3. Allow yourself to feel the emotions related to enlarging your multicultural experience and deepening relationships. These emotions can be anger, frustration, or guilt that will bubble up when you are on the receiving end of privilege. The emotions can also be joy and togetherness that will arise from engaging in multicultural relationships and taking action against any form of racism you witness.

4. You need to know the difference between that part of you that yearns to be the perfect "natural" White person, and the part of you that is committed to being a White anti-racist. Racism is real, as well as socialization. You won't always be a hundred percent anti-racist. Accept that you might fall short sometimes.

5. Remain calm as you discover the difficult things that are attached to white privilege, and learn to view them as an opportunity to learn more about your privileges. Don't get defensive when presented with these challenges. Get curious instead and let the desire for growth and understanding bubble up within you.

6. Take part in individual and collective protests against racism.

7. Value any personal analysis of your White identity.

8. Think about the racist thoughts you used to have and behaviors you used to portray, but do this with your current enlightenment so that you can better understand and alter those behaviors and thoughts in others.

Tema Okun believes that white people can adopt six responsibilities in the process of becoming anti-racist. When you choose to be anti-racist, you need to understand that it isn't a one-time decision or something you will ever completely achieve. It is a commitment. It's a choice that you need to make every day. Let's take a look at Tema's six responsibilities you have as an anti-racist.

Responsibilities of a White Anti-Racist

1. Read. Educate yourself on the impacts, structures, and effects of racism. Read as often as you can to stay updated.

2. Reflect. Do some self-reflection on what this enlightenment means to you as a White person choosing to be anti-racist. This reflection involves seeking out new ways to rebel against racism and working on initiatives for racial justice.

3. Keep in mind that you might participate in actions, thoughts, and beliefs that glorify racism, whether you mean to or not. There are days that you will forget the existence of racism, and will need to bring yourself

back and point out any internalized racist feelings you might have about people of color.

4. Be prepared to take risks that challenge racism whenever you recognize it or catch yourself engaging in it. Anytime you hear a racial stereotype, interrupt it. Also, openly stand with people of color in professional or personal settings when they recount their experiences with racism.

5. Make peace with rejection. It is an unavoidable experience as White racist because you are bound to make mistakes, especially when it involves recognizing and fighting racism. Sometimes, it might be difficult to understand how a decision, action, or even a sentence you make can be a trigger for people of color. This is a result of your white privilege. You will get rejected by people of color, and maybe even held accountable for the racial mistakes you made. Instead of choosing to be defensive, choose to understand, and embrace this rejection. You can't blame them because their anger is justified, and they're bound to reject white people in general harshly. When you are faced with this kind of rejection, you need to understand that it is a result of the unfair treatment of a racist system. So don't take it to heart; instead, help them if you can. Regardless, the fight against racism continues.

6. Building multicultural relationships are part of your responsibilities on your journey to anti-racism. Link up with fellow anti-racist white people and people of color who are open to having you in their community and themselves in yours.

How to be Anti-Racist as a Person of Color

People of color can also be anti-racist, despite being the victims of racism. This involves being conscious of racism and race as it exists in the world, and a dedication to voice and act against racism whenever they experience it. Do you remember the first stage of racial identity development for people of color? It is the obliviousness about the existence of racism, and this stage lasts until they encounter or are victims of an overt act of racism. As soon as they achieve this awareness, it is very common for them to lean towards having negative feelings about White people, and sometimes, people of other races as well.

You will be challenging this sort of racist behavior if you claim and live by the code of anti-racism. You may have come across incidents where Asians reacted in a racially biased manner towards Black people, and vice versa. Over the years, Black people have learned very little about Asian culture, except that Asians are foreign and most likely a threat. This is even worse for Asians who have a hard time speaking English and still maintain their culture despite being so far away from home.

Cultivating an anti-racist mentality as a person of color means that acknowledging the struggles of other races one way or another under white supremacy. It means acknowledging that the oppressed races do not always stand together in solidarity under a big umbrella labeled 'people of color.' Misinformation, bias, and violence can exist between other colored races and need immediate confrontation as much as white racism. Anti-racism as a person of color means being informed of the enslavement and immigration histories of other races besides your own. It also means acknowledging important class differences that affect the degree of oppression, even among people in your race.

You can practice anti-racism by taking action and challenging internalized white supremacy. You do this by interrupting the patterns that reveal racial prejudice amongst people of color. You can choose to challenge statements made by someone at work or home. In doing so on an institutional and personal level, you create a sense of community with other racial groups, while recognizing the differences in the expression of racism across said groups.

Also, there's the possibility of creating a collective movement against racism on multiple systemic and individual levels. One way of doing this is to have conversations with people from other affected racial groups and identify the similarities between the racial bias across groups. This way, you can stand together against white supremacy as a larger community.

Different Ways To Be Antiracist

The following are six stages you can follow:

1) Understand the meaning of racist.

Discussions about racism regularly endure when members can't characterize the importance of the word. Merriam-Webster portrays racism as "a conviction that race is the essential determinant of human attributes and limits and that racial differences produce an inalienable prevalence of a specific race." Few individuals would concede that definition mirrors their perspectives, yet all things considered deliberately or accidentally have faith in or underwrite racist thoughts.

Kendi goes further, characterizing the word racist as: "One who is supporting a racist strategy through their activities or inaction or communicating a racist thought." This sharp definition powers the peruser to consider themselves responsible for their thoughts and activities. An antiracist composes Kendi is "One who is supporting an antiracist approach through their activities or communicating an antiracist thought."

2) Stop saying, "I'm not racist."

It's insufficient to state, "I'm not racist," and frequently, it's a self-serving opinion. Kendi says individuals continually change the meaning of what's racist, so it doesn't concern them. On the off chance that you're a white patriot who's not savage, says Kendi, at that point, you may see the Ku Klux Klan as racist. In case you're a Democrat who believes there's something socially wrong with dark individuals, at that point, racists to you may be individuals who are Republicans.

In this way, for instance, in case you're a white liberal who sees herself as "not racist," however you won't send your kid to a nearby government-funded school because the populace is dominatingly African American, that decision is racist. The antiracist position would be to, at any rate, consider enlisting your kid or potentially finding out about the inconsistencies and disparities influencing that school to battle them.

3) Identify racial imbalances and differences.

Racism yields racial imbalances and aberrations in each segment of private and open life. That remembers for legislative issues, human services, criminal equity, instruction, salary, work, and home possession. Being antiracist implies finding out about and recognizing imbalances and aberrations that give, specifically, white individuals, or any racial gathering, material focal points over non-white individuals.

At the point when Social Security was made in 1935, for instance, it prohibited residential and horticultural laborers, most of whom were dark. While the Social Security Administration denies racial predisposition was a factor in that choice, it despite everything implied that colored laborers had less open door through the span of decades to collect investment funds and riches contrasted with white specialists. Different strategies that excessively gave "charge financed riches building openings" to white Americans created comparative outcomes for dark Americans. So a racist examination would attribute poor or more regrettable results for colored Americans to the gathering's conduct or qualities. An antiracist investigation would clarify that the issue isn't the gathering; however, the approaches that put racial meetings at a distinct drawback.

4) Confront the racist thoughts you've held or kept on holding.

When you've started distinguishing racial differences, look at whether your perspectives, convictions, or casting ballot designs have legitimized racial disparity. In case you're the parent who won't send a youngster to a transcendently dark school, consider how that decision impacts your perspectives on discipline approaches and contract schools, the arrangement gives that are profoundly interwoven with race and racism. Do you vote in favor of educational committee or city board up-and-comers who would prefer not to address instructive aberrations or neutralize nearby supporters attempting to increment informative value? Do you realize that subsidizing arrangements influence how assets are allotted to schools and why those practices can make racial variations? To numerous individuals, these real factors most likely appear to be separated from whether they're racist. However, Kendi contends that staying uninformed about them, or declining to change strategies that produce inconsistencies, isn't a possibility for somebody who needs to be antiracist.

Kendi's excursion shows that individuals can hold racist thoughts without acknowledging they're one-sided — and keeping in mind that they grasp antiracist ideas. On the off chance that you don't know whether your convictions or perspectives are racist, tune in to forefront racial equity backers, activists, and associations that have laid out antiracist positions and arrangements. Let that listening brief further reflection concerning why you've had faith in specific thoughts.

5) Understand how your antiracism should be intersectional.

Kendi contends that racist thoughts and strategies target a wide range of individuals inside racial gatherings. A plan that makes disparity among white and Native American individuals, for instance, likewise yields an imbalance between white men and Native American ladies. If one accepts that dark men are better than dark ladies, at that point, that individual won't have the option to perceive how specific thoughts and strategies excessively influence dark ladies in unsafe manners.

Since race converges with various parts of individuals' personalities, including their sex, sexuality, and ethnicity, it's essential to utilize an intersectional approach while being antiracist.

6) Champion antiracist thoughts and strategies.

One can't endeavor to be antiracist without activity, and Kendi says that a single direction to act is by supporting associations in your locale that are battling approaches that make racial differences. You can chip in for or finance those associations. Kendi likewise suggests utilizing one's capacity or getting into a place of ability to change racist approaches in any setting where they exist — school, work, government, etc. The fact of the matter is to focus on some type of activity that can change racist approaches.

Tema Okun also has a list of responsibilities that should accompany you on the journey to anti-racism as a person of color. However, I will modify it a little to accommodate the examination of any biases you may have internalized about other people of color. Let's take a look at Tema's six anti-racist responsibilities for people of color.

Responsibilities of a Colored Anti-Racist

1. Ensure that you are educated and updated on the effects, structures, and impacts of racism, not only on your racial group but on others as well.

2. Take some time to reflect on this education and what it means to you as a person of color, developing a racist mentality.

3. Keep in mind that you might be engaging in actions, thoughts, and beliefs that glorify racism knowingly or unknowingly. Point out these negative feelings that may have internalized about other people of color.

4. Consider how you have been complicit with racism when a racist incident is taking place. Think about all the times you didn't, and still don't, speak for yourself and other people of color.

5. Don't pass up an opportunity to challenge racism when you recognize it or realize that you are engaging in it against other people of color.

6. Make efforts to understand the anger that you may harbor about racism. Reject racism from white people, as well as other races when that happens. Continue to fight against racial bias with a complete understanding of the disadvantages or privileges you may experience compared to other people of color.

It is alright to be upset about racism. Your anger is justified by the pain it has caused you, and so many others in your community. However, it is more productive to channel all that energy into the fight against racism, which includes holding the perpetrators accountable for their racist acts. Just so we are clear, generally speaking, it is not your job to ensure that racists are made to account for their actions, but it is a vital part of being anti-racist as a person of color. Remember that you may also have some internalized stereotyped notions about your community, so be on the lookout for the manifestation of these attitudes and join forces with others in your community to drop all that negativity in the bin.

Chapter 5: Combating racism and xenophobia

Measures to Combat Various Forms of Racism and Xenophobia

People across the EU continue to be targeted for racism, xenophobia, and other forms of intolerance only because of their race. Skin color, religion, national or ethnic origin or origin, sexual orientation or gender identity, disability, social status, or other properties.

The EU rejects and condemns all forms of racism and intolerance because they are incompatible with the values and principles that the EU is founded.

There is a comprehensive set of rules at the EU level that helps to better address the different forms and manifestations of racism and racism Intolerance, especially the framework decision to combat certain forms of racism and xenophobia by the media of criminal law.

Relevant parts of EU legislation to combat racism, xenophobia and other types of intolerance are:

1. The Victims' Rights Directive, which sets minimum standards for the rights, support, and protection of all victims. With special attention

to victims who have committed a crime with prejudice or discriminatory motives.

2. The Audiovisual Media Services Directive, which prohibits hate speech in audiovisual media services and on the Internet Promotion of discrimination in audiovisual commercial communication.

3. Non-discrimination legislation, particularly the Racial Equality Directive, which prohibits discrimination due to race or ethnic origin in different areas of life and the equality directive that prohibits this Discrimination for various reasons in the field of employment

4. Legislation prohibiting discrimination in border controls Building on the existing legal framework, the EU has launched a wide range of measures to prevent and Combat Racism, xenophobia, and other forms of intolerance.

These measures are intended to support national authorities and civil society in intensifying preventive and countermeasures the spread of bigotry and hate, better enforcement of discrimination, hate crime and hate speech laws against victims. The necessary support, and support awareness-raising, improving data collection and monitoring trends.

Collection and exchange of information

The European Commission facilitates the exchange of information and best practices across various networks and expert groups.

In particular, the EU high-level group on combating racism, xenophobia and other forms of intolerance, on which is based The previous technical cooperation between the European Commission and the EU countries were set up as part of the European Commission Your commitment to improving responses to hatred and intolerance in the EU after the 2015 annual colloquium Fundamental rights.

Other relevant platforms for exchange and collaboration are;

- EU-Israel seminars to combat anti-Semitism, racism, and xenophobia within the framework of EU-Israel measures to plan

- Six-monthly roundtables with NGOs working against hatred and discrimination against Muslims.

- The high-level EU group on non-discrimination, equality, and diversity

The European Commission also supports and works closely with the EU Agency for Fundamental Rights (FRA) collects and analyzes data and conducts research on fundamental rights and offers support and experience in the EU and national level, including in the areas of non-discrimination, racism, bigotry and hate crime.

Specific measures to combat hate online

In addition to measures to prevent and combat racism, xenophobia, and other forms of intolerance, the EU is also committed to this Prevent and combats the spread of hate online.

Online hate speech not only hurts certain groups and individuals but also prevents citizens from expressing themselves for freedom. Tolerance and non-discrimination in the online environment have a deterrent effect on online democratic discourse Platforms.

The European Commission's actions in this area aim to protect freedom of expression by helping users to express themselves freely their opinions online without fear of being attacked by prejudices based on race, color, religion, race, nationality or nationality ethnic origin, sexual orientation and gender identity, disability or other characteristics. It also aims to ensure that the EU National anti-hate speech legislation is best applied online across the EU.

Among the most important measures in this area, the European Commission approved Facebook, Microsoft,

Twitter, and YouTube Code of conduct to combat illegal hate speech online. To help users report illegal hate speech on social platforms, you should improve support for civil society as well as for civil society Coordination with the national authorities. The European Commission is closely monitoring progress in the implementation of the Code and reports regularly on its activities in this area.

Financial support

The European Commission provides financial support to national authorities and civil society in this area.

Equality and citizenship programs

Other programs offer funding in areas that can help combat racism, xenophobia, and racism. Other forms of intolerance:

- The safest Internet programs to protect children using the Internet and other communication technologies to Example fight against racist and xenophobic content

- Lifelong learning programs to promote cultural diversity, democratic values, and respect for human rights.

- Migration and Integration Fund to facilitate the integration of third-country nationals by Asylum.

Racism occurs between individuals, at an interpersonal level, and is embedded in organizations and institutions through its Policies, procedures, and practices. In general, it appears to be easier to identify individual or interpersonal racist acts.

"Individual" racism does not arise in an empty, but arises from the basic beliefs of a society and "ways" to see/do things, and manifests itself in Organizations, institutions, and systems (including education). Here are some useful difficulties:

Individual racism refers to an individual's racist beliefs, beliefs or behavior and is "a form of racial discrimination that results from personal prejudices, problems, and loss of consciousness ". Individual racism is connected to learned/learned from broader socio-economic stories and processes and supported and reinforced by systemic racism.

Because we live in a culture of individualism (and with the privilege of freedom of expression), some people argue that your statements/ideas are not racist because they are only "personal opinions". Here it is important to note how Individualism is working to erase hierarchies of power and connect unrecognized personal ideologies with large racial groups or the systemic (i.e. individualism can be used as a defense reaction). It is therefore important to understand the system Racism and how it works.

Systemic racism includes the policies and practices anchored in established institutions that are excluded or taken into account the promotion of designated groups. It differs from open discrimination in that no individual intent is necessary.

It manifests in two ways:

1. Institutional Racism*:* racial discrimination that stems from people who dictate others with prejudice or a society with prejudice

2. Structural Racism*:* inequalities that are based on the functioning of society in the whole system and exclude significant amounts of racism and members of private groups with significant participation in the main social institutions.

Some Canadian examples of systemic racism are the poll tax of 1885, the Exclusion Act of 1923, the Refugee Women Act of 1897, Approved in Ontario, which penalized "immoral" and "incorrigible" acts of women if it was found to be pregnant illegitimate or drunk in public.

Other forms or manifestations of systemic racism may not be as obvious to some, including those privileged by the EU.

Fortunately, people can be anti-racist within and despite systematic racist systems and institutions.

The physical and mental effects of racism

Belonging to a minority exposed to racism can adversely affect a person's physical and/or mental health.

Health

Institutional racism can also limit access to high-quality care for people from minority groups and increase their risk for various health problems. For example, in 1988 the Centers for Disease Control and Prevention (CDC) found large differences in child mortality between black and white infants. For white babies, the mortality rate was 8.5 per 1,000 births, while the mortality rate for black babies was 17.6 per 1,000 births.

Stress

On a personal level, racism can negatively affect a person's physical and mental health by causing additional stress. For example, 18.2% of respondents who are black reported emotional stress compared to only 3.5% of white participants. Stress increases the risk of many illnesses, including Depression, colds, seasonal diseases, heart diseases, and cancer. Dealing with chronic stress can also lead to health problems Health options such as tobacco, alcohol, or drug use.

Chapter 6: Concept that you should know and teach your children

There are some concepts and realities that you should be aware of as a conscious and aware person in general, but as a parent in particular. To create an informed conversation with your children, you have to be, well, informed. As I have mentioned before, you don't need to know everything to teach it to your children, you can also discover things together, it will make for a beautiful, rewarding journey. But there are some realities and some structural problems that you should be aware of if you intend to raise anti-racist children.

The keywords for systematic racism before we move along.

Normalization means that structural racism is built into everyday practice.

We're not talking about exceptional behavior, individual bad attitudes.

We're not talking about the occasional negatively intentional policy.

We're talking about a process that happens in a normal way that goes on as part of our air that we breathe, but that is often quite invisible to us -not all of us but to some of us.

But it's important to know that it can go on while we're sleeping, while we're fighting for justice, while we're doing whatever we're doing.

Legitimization is important because we legitimize institutions -and I'm going to talk later about how this happens- that is functioning in structurally racist ways.

The outcomes are producing dramatic cumulative and chronic adverse outcomes. And they nonetheless have quite a legitimacy. They have a lot of legitimacy. This is not something that is marginal again and on the side.

The second piece of the definition that's important is that structural racism is not just the past that has a legacy that's waning in the present. It has a present formulation. So, it's historical, yes. But it's also present tense. There are cultural elements to it. That means it has to do with the way we talk about race that helps produce it. It's not just policies. But it is institutions and policies. We see it in government policy. We see it in corporations in their policies. We see it in educational institutions. And of course, it is also interpersonal.

There are critical areas that we will focus on where structural racism is highly dynamic and consequential. There are others: housing, education, mass media, wealth, and jobs are just critical fundamental anchors.

The outcomes in these areas determine fundamentally the quality of life, the sense of safety and security, and the opportunity that our citizens in this country have.

Whether it's educational outcomes or the criminal justice system, we tend to look at these things in isolation from one another. And this is not a bad idea when we want to drill down because, if you want to look at the significance of, say, racialized wealth inequality, which is dramatic and I'll point that out later, you want to figure out why and how. So, you have to go down and into it. You have to keep moving in more deeply. But at the same time, it's extremely important to think about how these gears, as we're thinking of them, work together. And they are not operating in a single sphere way, that there are interlocking effects. And this is key to the argument of systemic racism. This is key to the approach to the institutionalized racism on which our country was built on; therefore, we must think about how various aspects of society produce structural inequalities in ways that are interdependent, interactive, and compounding. And this is extremely important because, again, if we find a disparity in, say, job discrimination or unemployment, there's a tendency to say, well, if we just fix that, we're good, right?

But if you look at the interlocking effects and you come to the realization that, in any one sphere, you have discrimination and inequality past, present and in policy and thinking and it's driving inequality in other areas, you can't possibly think in a single sphere way to solve any given problem that we're dealing with.

So, we're making an argument that it's not just structural in the big picture sense in isolated ways, but it's interlocking and interdependent.

So how structural racism is made invisible? The first is this obsession with the illusion of meritocracy. Now, let me first say that the fact that we do not have a meritocracy, in my opinion, does not mean that people don't deserve good jobs, which they haven't worked hard, that they're not smart. It means that the system is structured for some people's work to matter a lot more than other people's hard work, and therefore it's not a functional meritocracy.

If meritocracy is that rewards in society go naturally to those who are the best performers and that positions or achievements of individuals depend on their abilities and effort and does not depend on class race or other group advantages, then obviously we're not a functional meritocracy. We have lots of merits. We try, but we do functionally fail.

This is very important to confront because it is the myth of this meritocracy that helps drive our misguided thinking about race in the first place. So inside of the meritocracy myth is the belief that we ended racism with the civil rights movement.

There's also tremendous evidence for significant hiring discrimination even at entry level jobs.

There is a profoundly limited accessible opportunity based on distance, transportation, and housing, segregation and isolation, and social networks. Almost all jobs are social networks.

These are two different spaces, but they're both important.

There are things people say that they think to be true, and then there are things that we don't even know about. 80% of our brain is completely inaccessible to us. Well, I don't know what's going on down there in that basement. But it's pretty heavy.

One of the things going on is a deep belief that black people are more criminal. And this starts really with the moment of emancipation. As soon as slavery ends - during slavery, black people are not criminal. But magically, as soon as they're free, they're pretty dangerous and problematic. Well, recent studies, though, show that whites overestimate the actual share of burglaries, illegal drug sales, and juvenile crime committed by African-Americans by 20% to 30%.

If this pattern is confirmed in widespread implicit bias research, media crime coverage reinforces this bias. There are many reports that show that the way black criminals are portrayed, the emphasis on crimes that are more likely to be done by blacks but not by others produce a reinforced relationship between black people and crime in the psyche. It's reinforced by higher sales and status for movies, music, and art that revolves around African-Americans' criminal behavior and character. In hip hop, for example, artists that don't talk about being a gangster do not sell as well. And it's not just because those stories are more exciting. It's because they fulfill a conscious and unconscious sense of authenticity about what black people are supposed to be. And it justifies draconian policing policies, and most important for what I want to do next, it drives housing and schooling decisions.

If you take the housing gear, you will see that there are lots of policies, past and present, which have had a deep impact on what we have always seen in the housing arena, which is significant segregation and significant economic disempowerment. I have already mentioned it in the first chapter.

So, just for the sake of recapping: there was a government policy New Deal.

So democratic, so don't get all grumpy if you're a Democrat trying to blame somebody else. The democratic policy meant to help communities be funded for housing and it was racially specific and it was a corporate collaboration because of the homeowner loan corporation founded by the government. It created a color-coded system.

We call it redlining because neighborhoods that were considered red and a red perimeter was circled them, they were neighborhoods where many black people lived even only one were marked in red was given the lowest rating on the system and ruled completely ineligible for home or business loans.

This went on and it is going on consistently across the country uninterrupted, and this is just one piece of the puzzle creating some extremely important factors.

Not only is it starving black communities of economic resources. It's elevating the wider the community is.

It's creating a financial incentive for white homogeneity.

This is very important because in itself produces thinking about race because, well, whiteness has value.

So redlining and other strategies that maintain segregation. They choked off the value of any investment in black communities and suppressed the value of the property.

Gentrification as we know it today is impossible without the history of redlining and the destruction of value in poor communities that they should have been able to access but can't, and now others find the prices to be so cheap because this process been going on. So, it created black ghettos by redlining and constraining and segregating neighborhoods and creating asset reduction in those communities. It reinforced associations of blackness with poverty and struggling community, artificially raised the value of white neighborhoods in a higher market value, which in turn fuels educational inequality and segregation.

As we all know, we fund -for those of us who still send our kids to public schools, that's a whole other racial and class effort to create segregation. But taxes fund our educational units, and therefore if you have higher property values for your house, you have more money for your schools. So, there's an incentive to pass this on intergenerational wealth through education alone, not to mention passing on these homes to our children. Which does what? Funds their college.

Weather financial crisis, weather health crises. If you don't have excellent health coverage for some reason and your child is doing some entrepreneurship, you can cover their health. You can pay for it with second mortgages with that wealth gap that I've mentioned - remember, $11,000 in assets to $142,000 on average.

It rationalizes white protectionism, protecting white neighborhoods as safer and profitable. It makes the fear of black people financially reasonable. It stigmatizes neighborhoods that are diverse no matter how safe, friendly, or stable. It fuels white self-segregation and white flight.

This whole logic -the perception, the bias, the history, the structures, the investments in whiteness- have created a context in which 20% functions as a tipping point that initiates the process of white flight. If you're living in a neighborhood that's less than 20% black, whites will move into that neighborhood, fewer than 20%.

But any more than 20% and the first thing that happens is whites stop moving in.

If it's more than 30%, whites sell their homes and move out. As you can see, if you think about this, this process creates segregation in and of itself. So, it doesn't take long that, when whites stop moving in, other people have to. Somebody moves in. It ends up being nonwhites. The neighborhood eventually becomes all people of color. So, this process can happen individually. And that means there's a deep investment in not being caught in this bigger than 30%

neighborhood because we know what the economic consequences that the market produces will be.

This is a normalized, legitimized project that happens historically and interpersonally and institutionally, that routinely advantages whites by providing a cumulative and chronic adverse outcome.

Now let's see how structural racism works in the context of life and a community. And for this, I've chosen a well-known case: the story of Trayvon Martin. Let's briefly review what happened.

Trayvon Martin was a black 17-year-old who was killed by a man named George Zimmerman on a Sunday night in February of 2012 while walking back to his father's house in Florida. Trayvon's death and Zimmerman's murder trial both received extensive media attention, most of which centered on Zimmerman's possible motivations and Trayvon's character. Most media focused on the micro details to explain what happened instead of focusing on the larger structural forces that set the stage for this tragedy. The cover that People Magazine ran after Trayvon's death reads "an unarmed 17-year-old is killed in a Florida neighborhood. How a chance encounter turned deadly, leaving a family devastated and a country outraged."

Now, that caption may seem innocuous to you, but it's hugely significant because it captures the core framing, the nearly universal common sense thinking about this case, and recent others like it.

People Magazine called the confrontation between Trayvon Martin and George Zimmerman a chance encounter. And in some ways, this is true. But on another level, this encounter wasn't random at all. What I want to illuminate is that, despite widespread media framing that suggested otherwise, the deadly encounter between Trayvon and Zimmerman was significantly shaped by structural racism. I want to talk in particular about how structural racism and the ideas about black people that justify it shape their encounter in three key areas-- in housing, in criminal justice, and schools.

In each of these areas, evidence of structural racism was largely ignored or misinterpreted through the lens of racial stereotypes and individual behavior. And I also want to show that the factors that shaped Trayvon Martin's life and death are by no means specific only to him or to his community. They're, instead, key components of how structural racism works in the United States.

Trayvon was shot while walking back to his father's girlfriend's home at the retreat at Twin Lakes, a lower-middle-class gated community in Sanford, Florida.

Zimmerman lived at Twin Lakes, and he was the captain of the community's neighborhood watch program. So, what kind of neighborhood was Zimmerman watching? And why was he watching it? Sanford is a city of about 50,000 in northern Florida, about 30 minutes from Orlando.

Both the city of Sanford and the retreat at Twin Lakes are fairly diverse places. Sanford is about 60% white and 30% black, and Twin Lakes is about 50% white, 20% Latinx, and 20% black. And Sanford has a median household income of about $38,000. So, we're talking about a lower- middle-class area, which is significant in part because Twin Lakes was built as an aspirational luxury oasis. The promotional video for Twin Lakes says "secluded gated community, is like living in a resort, the perfect choice for those looking for space and comfort".

In 2004, when Twin Lakes was built, a 4,500 square foot townhouse went for $250,000. But in retrospect, 2004 was part of what we would now call the housing bubble and was a very bad time to build a gated community of aspirational luxury townhouses. A few years later, the Great Recession hit. The housing market collapsed, and many residents as well as new investors in Twin Lakes started renting their properties to cover their mortgages. By 2012, in a pattern that repeated itself around the country, the same townhouse that was worth $250,000 eight years earlier was now worth under $100,000. So in 2012, the retreat at Twin Lakes is a community on an emotional edge. But it was also on another kind of edge.

As I have explained, due to whites' negative racial perceptions of black people, whites stop moving into a neighborhood once it's above 20% black and move out of neighborhoods that are over 30% black. So, the retreat at Twin Lakes, which is 20% black and located in Sanford, which is 30% black sat right on the threshold where whites have decided a neighborhood is becoming too black or not white enough. And this racial tipping point, as you recall, has economic consequences. Because of the higher market value attached to white neighborhoods, white flight accelerates declines in property values, which in turn leads to more white flight. White flight stems in part from whites unfounded, yet widespread, hyper-association with black people as criminals. And Twin Lakes demonstrated this ideology in textbook fashion.

In the 14 months before Zimmerman killed Trayvon Martin, there were an estimated 45 burglaries or attempted burglaries at Twin Lakes. Reuters reported that, of those 45, only three were known to be carried out or attempted by black men. In the summer of 2011, the summer before Zimmerman killed Trayvon, there was a small wave of burglaries at Twin Lakes, including a particularly well-publicized one where a mother and her child had to lock themselves in a room while two burglars ransacked their home. Without any statistical evidence to back up their claims, residents talking to reporters in the aftermath of the killing of Trayvon Martin described a community besieged by black criminals.

One neighbor said quote, "there were black boys robbing houses in the neighborhood." That's why George was suspicious of Trayvon Martin. Another resident told a different reporter that neighborhood burglaries were being committed primarily by quote "young black males." in the fall of 2011, just after this small wave of robberies, Twin Lakes decided to form a neighborhood watch. And George Zimmerman volunteered to be the captain.

In many ways, though, George Zimmerman had already been the unofficial watchdog of this gated community. He moved into Twin Lakes in 2009. And in the two-plus years between when he moved in and when he killed Trayvon, Zimmerman called the police incessantly to report all sorts of things. But during the summer of 2011, the focus of Zimmerman's calls to police narrowed significantly, specifically, the Tampa Bay Times reported, "He started to fixate on black men he thought looked suspicious."

Often this was reported as an individual fixation of Zimmerman's. And it may really have been one, but Zimmerman's behavior embodied an irrational racial paranoia that appeared to be widespread at Twin Lakes and is certainly widespread around the country.

So, you have a neighborhood which has been made fragile by the financial housing sector, and one that is made additionally fragile because of the market penalties attached to a diverse neighborhood, sitting right on what, for whites, is that crucial 20% racial tipping point, a point that activates white racial anxiety.

And in Zimmerman, you have a resident who has been operationalizing this racial anxiety, who also has an intimate knowledge of the racial dimensions of housing values thanks to a career spent in real estate and working for a mortgage company, who then volunteers to be the captain of the neighborhood watch and sees a black teenager walking through the gated community alone on a Sunday night. Zimmerman pursues Trayvon in his car, and then eventually gets out and confronts him even though the police dispatch he called specifically instructed him not to approach Trayvon at all. Zimmerman chases Trayvon. And when he catches him, the two of them struggle. And then Zimmerman shoots and kills Trayvon Martin.

He admits this to the police immediately when they arrive. Trayvon was unarmed, and it's clear from the 911 transcripts that Zimmerman instigated the encounter. And yet Zimmerman isn't charged with any crime. Police take a statement, and they let him go home. And it's during the six weeks that Zimmerman goes uncharged that this killing becomes national news. It wasn't just that Zimmerman shot Trayvon. It was that he had done it, admitted to it, and then been allowed to walk free.

Why did Zimmerman go uncharged for a month and a half? Well, there are a lot of ways that the killing of black people has been excused and legitimized. But one reason was that Zimmerman was able to invoke a new Florida law called Stand Your Ground, a law that was created in 2005 with the support of the NRA and gun retailers and is now law in some form in 33 states.

Stand Your Ground extends what's called the castle doctrine. Since basically the beginning of its existence, the United States has had the castle doctrine, as in a man's home is his castle, which is adapted from English Common Law. It essentially says that, if there is an intruder in your home, you're allowed to kill that person even if it's possible for you to escape.

A century ago, Judge Benjamin Cardozo, who later became a Supreme Court Justice, described the castle doctrine like this - a man quote "if assailed at home, may stand his ground and resist the attack. He is under no duty to take to the fields and the highways, a fugitive in his own home."

What Stand Your Ground did was widely expand the castle doctrine.

Under Stand Your Ground, anyone who's attacked, anywhere he or she is lawfully present has quoted "no duty to retreat and has the right to stand his or her ground and meet force with force, including deadly force, if he or she reasonably believes that it's necessary to do so to prevent death or great bodily harm." So, before the castle doctrine allowed the lethal force to protect people inside their homes. Now, in states that have passed Stand Your Ground, we allow it wherever someone is legally present. Your castle is now anywhere you happen to be and your reasonable belief in your danger can justify killing another person. But is this reasonable belief standard race-neutral? Let's look at some of the data.

Killing will be deemed justified based on the race of the shooter and the victim, using white on white killings as the zero baselines. So, a black person killing a black person is less likely to be seen as justified. And a black person killing a white person is far less likely to be seen as justified compared to a white person who kills a white person.

When whites kill black people, they are 2 and 1/2 times more likely to be seen as justified. And in Stand Your Ground states, that number is even bigger.

Whites are 3 and 1/2 times more likely to be found justified if they kill a black person instead of a white one.

Put in the language of the law itself, white on black killings in Stand Your Ground states are significantly more likely to be seen as stemming from a reasonable fear, the kind of fear that George Zimmerman invoked when he chased, confronted, and killed an unarmed Trayvon Martin.

Now legally, Stand Your Ground was not supposed to be part of Zimmerman's defense trial because both sides agreed that the details of the physical struggle between him and Trayvon made the law inapplicable. But it didn't need to serve its purpose. The media talked so much about Stand Your Ground as a mitigating factor, and the defense used the phrase to stand your ground repeatedly during the argument. And so, it appears that jurors, whose racial bias were no different than anyone else's, were confused and used the racially inflicted logic of Stand Your Ground anyway. After the verdict, one juror told CNN that the jury did acquit Zimmerman in part because of Stand Your Ground which exposed a shocking misunderstanding of the law's role in the case, but a keen sense of its role in our society. And one of the tragic ironies of this killing is that, while Trayvon fell victim in Sanford to one kind of criminalization, he was there in part to escape another kind of criminalization.

Trayvon didn't live primarily in Sanford. He lived and went to school in Miami four hours south. The night he was killed was a school night, but Trayvon was in Sanford with his father because he had been suspended from school and didn't need to be back in Miami the next morning.

The suspension that led Trayvon to stay in Sanford with his dad was his third of the year. His first was for tardiness. His second was for writing the acronym WTF on a walker, and his third was for possessing a bag that had marijuana residue on it.

Now, this might seem to you to be cut and dry. Trayvon broke the rules, and so he was suspended. And his suspension was often cited in the media as proof of troubling behavior.

But it's quite a bit more ambiguous than that. Krop High, Trayvon's school, has detailed guidelines for which offenses warrant which types of punishment. Now, these guidelines themselves are quite draconian, but even if we set that aside for now, it's clear from the details of Trayvon's suspensions that he was treated unfairly even by his school's zone standards.

According to the school own guidelines, Trayvon's first two offenses shouldn't have resulted in suspensions at all. For his third, he got the maximum suspension for an offense that appears to be one of the least serious drug offenses possible.

So, by punishing him excessively and against the established rules, his school created a pattern of offenses which then snowballed and justified a stiff penalty for the one actual offense.

Now, the tricky thing about looking at structural racism through the lens of one student's suspensions is that there is a lot of ambiguity and subjectivity involved. We can say for sure that Trayvon's first two suspensions weren't warranted, but there may be additional context we simply don't know about.

But when we put Trayvon in a larger context, we see some worrisome patterns. Since the 1970s, the percentage of students suspended from school has doubled, and black students have been suspended disproportionately. Today, black students are suspended at three times the rate of white students and twice as often as Latinx students.

The most heavily suspended students are black, male, and disabled. And black students aren't just over suspended. They're also judged more punitively for the same behavior when compared to their peers of other races. In Okaloosa County, where Krop is located, roughly 50% of school arrests involve black students, even though they make up only 12% of the school population.

At Krop High, Trayvon's school specifically, the data is similar. Nearly 50% of Krop suspensions are given to black students who account for only under a quarter of the student population as a whole.

This is one of the key ways structural racism works. It posits that racial disparities are the product not of systems, but black individuals' behavior and then primes people to search for evidence of behavior that can account for the disparity. This erasure of the workings of structural racism and the use of behaviorally focused racial stereotyping was present in all of the other issues I have mentioned.

Let's take a quick look at some of the headlines from stories about the case to get a sense of the pattern.

NBC says Trayvon Martin suspended from school three times.

New York Magazine says FBI sources say George Zimmerman isn't racist.

USA Today, Trayvon Martin typical teen or troublemaker?

CBS, George Zimmerman used a racial slur in a bar.

And the New York Times says defense in the Trayvon Martin case raises questions about the victim's character.

All of these headlines draw our attention to questions of individual behavior as a way of explaining what happened, and they draw our attention away from important racially discriminatory forces and perceptions.

What I hope I've conveyed today is that Trayvon Martin's death was the product of much more than what People Magazine called a chance encounter.

It was the product of structural racism in three key areas: in housing, it was the product of racialized fears about crime and neighborhood prosperity; in criminal justice, it was the product of a legal logic which legitimize the killing and demonized the victim; and in schools, it was the product of the racially targeted application of draconian school policy.

The micro-level, interpersonal details of these cases of course do matter. But the way we've explained what happened to Trayvon Martin hides how structural racism works and the damage it does.

Chapter 7: Mistakes Parents/Guardian make while Educating Kids

Many guardians converse with their kids about grasping contrast, however, in unobtrusive, secret ways, they convey something altogether different. For instance, when moving toward a gathering of dark youths, a mother may unknowingly pull the youngster closer to her. Likewise, numerous white guardians frequently converse with kids about the shades of malice of partiality and separation, yet in their possess lives they have scarcely any companions or neighbors of shading with whom they consistently mingle.

These verifiable correspondences are more impressive than any purposeful endeavors on the part of guardians.

Parents once in a while get excessively humiliated or self-cautious [with] children's inquiries about the distinction, particularly when those inquiries are posed openly. Guardians ought to treat them as fair requests, disclose it to them like a logical inquiry, and do whatever it takes not to consider them to be an awful thing because these inquiries are common. On the off chance that a kid poses an inquiry about somebody's earthy colored skin and the parent gets cautious or humiliated or attempts to brush the inquiry aside, that kid begins to relate that and believe, "Is there something terrible about earthy colored skin?"

Guardians of preschoolers appear to be all around educated about things like picking a protected sponsor seat of the vehicle or the significance of getting their adolescents to eat the best possible nourishments.

Frequently, race relations projects and exercises center on mindfulness and information about and conduct toward, people of shading. What's more, a portion of these projects centers on the treatment of and demeanor toward a solitary racial or ethnic gathering. Where racial and ethnic decent variety exists, assorted variety gives a chance to learning and for the correlation that can help maintain a strategic distance from misrepresentation or generalizing. Besides, whites have fluctuating societies and personalities. Bringing issues to light of this reality may serve to expand the refinement of the exercise being instructed and learned.

Racism is mental laziness

That is why it is not enough to leave education to school: the family has an important responsibility. No one is born racist, one becomes racist when models and education are wrong, and when thinking is guided by prejudices and stereotypes. Racism is the "easy" answer to the complexity that comes from difference. It is a way to accelerate reasoning, a cognitive saving, a "mental laziness" from which stereotypes arise, that is, generalized descriptions based on a few obvious characteristics, sometimes positive but most of the time negative.

How to fight this unjust mental laziness? For once with an easy and pleasant exercise. Illustrated albums! Beautiful, exciting, and engaging children's books that foster feelings of openness and empathy.

Experience diversity

Another way to educate children about diversity is to make them travel. Travel is a fundamental educational experience, so much so that this year the European Union has allocated 12 million euros to give thirty thousand girls and boys aged 18 years old the Inter-Rail pass that allows them to take all trains and ferries in Europe for free.

Of course, with young children, you don't improvise a trip to Africa, America or Asia, which are cradles of civilizations rich in culture and interesting traditions.

Different cultures can be known even without moving from home. There are theatre shows, parties, and events organized by social promotion associations that work to promote inter-culture. There are opportunities for music and food, sports and games where you can socialize with children from all over the world. Above all, there is our behavior, which must always be kept open and always available. Because if we want to raise good adults, we must be good first of all.

Why aren't we racist with little kids?

Our brains are programmed to take care of children up to the age of three, regardless of factors which, when they are adults, may be grounds for discrimination, such as the color of their skin.

We are not racist with small children because our brains are programmed to take care of them regardless of the color of their skin. This is the result of research conducted by the Bicocca University of Milan and published in Neuropsychology. When children grow up, i.e. after the age of three, the brain is instead conditioned by the so-called Other-race effect (Ore), the "regulating principle" according to which faces belonging to our ethnic group are more easily recognized.

Parental love

With the faces of infants (children between six months and three years), however, this mechanism does not happen. This is due to their physical conformation, i.e. the fact that they have a larger head than the body, big eyes, small nose and mouth, and chubby cheeks. The study has shown that when you come across this baby scheme there is a stimulation of the orbital-frontal region of the brain, where the "pleasure circuit" is located: it is from here that positive stimuli such as maternal or parental love arise.

Protection and survival

Alice Mado Proverbio, author of the research together with Valeria De Gabriele of the Department of Psychology of the University of Milano-Bicocca, said: "The data show how the human brain is programmed to take care of children of any ethnicity; this "racial" information is ignored by the brain if they are children, while it acts on the regulation of behavior (prejudice) if they are adults. The pleasure and tenderness that we spontaneously feel at the sight of small children (generalized to puppies of other species) is the result of an innate brain mechanism to ensure protection and survival to young non-breeding children, and indeed to any human ethnic group".

Chapter 8: Discrimination

Racial discrimination

What is racial discrimination? This is the case if you are treated differently due to your race in one of the situations. Treatment can be a one-time measure or the result of a race-based rule or policy. An item doesn't have to be intentional to be illegal.

The 2010 Gender Equality Act states that you shouldn't be discriminated against because of your race. In the Gender Equality Act, race can mean its skin color or its nationality (including its citizenship). It can also mean your ethnicity or national origin that may not match your current nationality. For example, you can have Chinese citizenship Origin and life in Great Britain with a British passport.

The race also includes ethnic and racial groups. This means a group of people who share the same protected feature ethnicity or race.

A race group can consist of two or more different race groups, for example, British Blacks, British Asians, British Sikhs, British Jews, Roma Gypsies, and Irish travelers.

Different types of racial discrimination

Direct Discrimination

This happens when your race treats you worse than someone in a similar situation. For example, if a rental agency would not rent an apartment to you based on your race, this would be direct racial discrimination.

Indirect Discrimination

This happens when an organization has a specific policy or way of working that brings people of your race group to a point of Disadvantage.

For example, a hairdresser refuses to hire stylists who cover their hair. This would put all Muslim women or Sikh men who put their hair at a disadvantage when they apply to be a stylist.

Indirect racial discrimination can sometimes be allowed if the organization or employer can show that it is a good reason for discrimination. This is called objective justification. For example, a Somali asylum seeker tries to open a bank account, the bank states that you must be resident in the UK for 12 years to be eligible Months and have a permanent address. The Somali cannot open a bank account. The bank would have to prove that their policy was necessary for business reasons (e.g. to prevent fraud) and there was no practical alternative.

Harassment

Harassment occurs when you feel humiliated, offended, or humiliated by someone.

For example, a young British-Asian man is repeatedly referred to as a racist name at work by colleagues. His colleagues say it's fair Joking, but the employee is offended and offended. Harassment can never be justified. However, if an organization or the employer can show that he has done everything to prevent people who work for him from behaving in this way. You won't be able to claim harassment, although you could claim the harasser.

Victimization

This is the case if you are treated badly because you have filed a complaint about racial discrimination under the Equal Opportunities Act. You may also support someone who has submitted a complaint about racial discrimination. For example, in the example above, the young man wants to file a formal complaint about his treatment. His manager threatens to fire him unless he drops the complaint. Circumstances if treated differently due to race are legal treatment can be legal in employment situations if: Belonging to a particular race is essential to hold a job in an organization.

This is known as a job requirement. For example, an organization would like to hire a worker to assist in a domestic violence counseling service for South Asian women. The organization can say that it only wants to employ someone with South Asian origin. An organization takes positive action to encourage or develop people in a race group that is underrepresented or disadvantaged in a role or activity. For example, a broadcaster hardly receives any applicants for its recruitment program for graduates from candidates from the Black Caribbean. It sets up a Work experience and mentoring program for Black Caribbean students to encourage them for the industry.

Opportunities to combat racism

- Rights and Identity

When someone is treated differently because of their race or culture, it can be referred to as racism. It can include things like calling people Name or exclusion and even refusal to serve in a company or things like job opportunities. It's illegal in the UK to discriminate (treat differently) because of their race.

If you or someone you know is experiencing racism, you can get help to stop this.

- Do not accept the Abuse

Everyone, regardless of nationality or race, has the right to live happily and free from discrimination. If you feel someone is racist about you. The main thing is to get away Stay safe and talk to someone you trust. You don't have to take revenge or react.

If someone is racist about you, your safety is the most important thing. If you feel vulnerable, stay with groups of friends you trust. If you or someone you know is in immediate danger or life-threatening, dial 999. Remember that you are not the one who is causing the problems. You have done nothing wrong.

- Keep Evidence

Keep a diary of what happened and keep text messages or messages to show others how it affects you and what support they provide you need. If you take action, any evidence you can collect will help your case.

- Tell Someone

Talk to your teachers, youth workers, friends and/or family members about what happens so they can get their help and Support for.

- Report It

You can report racist incidents to Police by visiting your local police station, filling out an online form.

When you report the incident, you should request it Incident reference number if you have problems speaking or understanding English or the local language, you can ask the police to provide you with an interpreter. They should provide you with one.

Remember: you don't have to be the race or culture that someone assumed to be when they say or do something to you to make it a crime or hate incident. Learn about hate crimes and incidents and how to report them.

- Stay Safe Online

If you experience abuse online, you can report it at any time using the "Report Abuse" button on most social media platforms.

Make sure your privacy settings are secure too. The UK's Safer Internet Center has some resources; including how to make sure each of your social media accounts is private and secure. You can also block people if they bother or intimidate you.

- Include Others

Talking only about racism is a big part of the fight. You can start an anti-racism project or newsletter on your website School/youth group or set up a discussion group to discuss relevant topics and what you can do to help.

- Never Give Up!

You may not be able to fight racism alone, but we can all participate. Defy racism when you see it (no exposing yourself to risk) and reporting it helps other people realize that it is wrong.

- Support Others

If you see or hear someone racist towards another person, you can support that person. You could help them report it if they want and offer to be a witness. This is called third-party reporting.

If you feel comfortable and the situation certainly means this, you can also challenge racism when you see him say you don't agree with that.

But each of us can endure every day against racial prejudice and intolerant attitudes.

Factors of Racial Discrimination

Ethnocentric

Racial discrimination based on ethnocentrism is based on the premise that men who are not in the "us" ethnic group belong to the "they" ethnic group, mainly if their lineage is doubtful or mixed with other races.

For example, in Spanish America, peninsular whites called Creole whites and shore whites to those whites who, having European descent, had been born in America and who had a lower social position than those born in the Old Continent.

Ideological

It is based on ideological precepts raised with philosophy. For example, during German fascism, Alfred Rosenberg considered Hitler's thinker, who wrote a treatise in which he claimed that the "Aryan race" was superior to the Jewish.

On the opposite side of the globe, Wetsuit Tetsuro argued in his book Fudo that Japan's natural environment had unique traits, which is why the Japanese were special beings with qualities that neither Chinese nor Koreans had.

Pseudoscientific

It came to be called "scientific racism" when it was in fashion between the 19th and 20th centuries. He used pseudoscience like phrenology to misrepresent evolutionary biology concepts to build thought models that promoted eugenics and "racial cleansing."

Only whites were thought to have a right to supremacy, and supposedly "scientific" evidence was available to demonstrate this view.

None of the postulates of "scientific racism" are true, and therefore unfounded. There is no evidence to support them. Therefore, this concept is discarded and superseded without any validity in current science.

Religious

Here religious criteria are used to cement racism. Alfred Rosenberg, mentioned above, suggested that all facets of Judaism or Semitic racial aspects should be erased from Christianity, since Jesus Christ was Aryan, German, and therefore European.

Mormonism is not far behind either. In his holy book, it is stated that God stipulates that good men are white, while bad men are blacks, who are the fruit of divine punishment.

Folkloric

This cause is rare, but it exists and there is evidence of it. It focuses, on racism that practices popular culture.

This happens a lot with the ethnic group of Dogons in Mali, who by oral tradition, fervently believe that a white, born child is a manifestation of evil spirits, and therefore must die. If he lives, he is the object of derision among his own, not knowing that such whiteness is due to a genetic condition called albinism.

Causes of Racial Discrimination

There are many causes of racial discrimination. Some of the most common are fear, ignorance, and prejudice, lack of information, or socio-economic circumstances. On many occasions, these reasons intermingle, even unconsciously, and lead to racist attitudes that violate human rights.

The first thing to end these causes is to know them, so let's go with the most common:

Fear

Much research agrees that the main cause of racism is fear. In 1968, a study carried out by psychologist Robert Zajonc proved that there is a close link between familiarity and our way of judging: the more we know something or someone, the more we like it, and vice versa. This popular idea is what is now called the Theory of the mere exposure effect.

Do you know the Doll test? It is a famous psychological experiment conducted in the United States in the 1940s to test the level of marginalization perceived by African American children due to discrimination, prejudice, and racial segregation. It was repeated in Italy in 2016 and the results showed that fear and prejudice towards other ethnic groups are still very present in our society. A boy or a girl, two dolls on the table, and some answers that will not leave you indifferent.

Ignorance

Closely linked to fear are ignorance and lack of information about other ethnic groups and cultures. Knowing, doubting, contrasting information and, above all, respecting diversity, are good tips to avoid racial discrimination. If you want to know more about this topic, we invite you to read on our blog about important issues, such as the difference between racism and xenophobia or types of racial discrimination. You can also make popcorn and enjoy these movies that will help you reflect on racism.

Socio-economic circumstances

The social and economic crises are also a breeding ground for discrimination. We have an example in Nazism. The disadvantageous result of Germany after the First World War left a country marked by poverty, inequality, and unemployment. One in four Germans had no job. The Nazi regime's promises of "bread and work," as well as propaganda aimed at blaming the Jewish people for all problems, brought many Germans together against a supposed common enemy to hate.

Ideology

Another frequent cause of racial discrimination is ideology. Throughout history, there have been currents of thought based on the segregation of people and the treatment of inferiority towards certain groups. These are ideologies that, today, are far from being eradicated.

Racial Zoning and Ghetto

Ghettos are places where large numbers of poor people live close to each other, often in rundown housing. There are White ghettos, Asian ghettos and Black ghettos where people of the same race, culture, or both, can be found.

Blacks in ghettos thus speak, think, dress, and live differently than suburban Whites, as well as suburban Blacks, because their culture deliberately intended to be different than White culture. A tight connection between race and religion develops when all of the people in a given area are of the same race or culture because being around like-minded people tends to reinforce certain types of behavioral tendencies among group members.

The cultural points of differentiation that group members develop serve to induce ghetto Blacks to look upon outsiders with contempt. The weaker they are, the more likely they are to see other ethnic, cultural, and racial groups in negative terms as a by-product of envy of those who have more than do, and the more likely they are to see their ethnic group as being important.

Ghettos And Crime

Whites often hear from the mass media about the astronomical unemployment rates in Black ghettos. These statistics, however, simply reflect the observable mainstream parts of the economy. When you factor in the "underground" parts of the economy, meaning the sort of criminal activities that are not including in the formal economics and unemployment statistics, you get a very different picture of the Black ghetto economy where criminals sprout up like weeds.

Most Whites are unaware that a large, difficult-to-measure, but real, percentage of Blacks in the ghetto have never had a real job in the sense of working nine-to-five for a paycheck in a factory, office or other formal organization. The reality is that these supposedly unemployed men and women work full time in underground-economy criminal activity "jobs" of the sort where a single offense can get them to put away for many years.

The only time that these career criminals get mainstream jobs was when they forced into work-release programs towards the end of their prison sentences. Once their work-release programs are over, they return to the same sort of underground-economy things in which they engaged before being locked up.

Black criminals who do not want to take chances on being locked up repeatedly do not stop being criminals after getting out of prison. They simply change their approach to crime to resemble the professional criminal procedure. They are telling lies in an attempt to control other people's money and property. They attempt to talk unsophisticated suckers into investing in bogus enterprises. They try to defraud addled widows out of their life savings and similar sorts of scams and hustles. Some also turn to attempt to convince Whites that they owe Blacks a living because of the "legacy of slavery," which is simply a ghetto hustle that targets Whites.

Ghetto residents who are not directly involved in crime in the sense of committing violent crimes such as robberies might be on the fringes of criminal activity. It can happen with ghetto residents who buy stolen property from thieves for cash. The primary form of economic activity that those who grow up in the ghetto hear about most often is not nine-to-five jobs but rather various types of career criminal activities. Crime is the social norm in the ghetto.

People who either already are, or are on their way to becoming career criminals, are obsessed with other people respecting them because they are criminals. Ghetto dropouts hate nonconformists who show that they can get ahead in any manner other than criminal activities.

That is why attending high school in the ghetto will get you laughed at and make you a target for attacks because staying in school makes dropouts, who constitute the majority of ghetto residents, look bad by comparison. High school dropout rates of fifty percent and more are standard in the ghetto.

Few ghetto residents know anybody with a real career other than in crime, so ghetto residents grow up thinking that finishing high school is a joke. They hear from other ghetto dropouts that they can make money in criminal activities of the sort conducted by gangs. The result is that ninety-eight percent of the residents of state prisons are gang members who are also ghetto high school dropouts. Dropping out of high school steers the dropout towards winding up either dead by age thirty in a gang war or ending up in the state prison with other dropouts.

Black men and women who drop out of high school have ninety percent of their lives written out in advance for them. The job market doesn't want them because they don't have any skills to offer the job market, and talk and dress in ways that are guaranteed to ensure that they are unwelcome outside the ghetto. Ghetto-style speech and clothing don't go over well in professional office environments.

Crime Is A Ghetto Career

Suburban Whites and Blacks who finish high school and college go on to get jobs in offices and factories. Ghetto dropouts are not welcome anywhere in the mainstream economy because they do not have the reading, writing, and mathematics skills necessary to compete with those who do have those skills. They turn to crime as a career because that is what everybody around them is doing, and they see few alternatives open to dropouts who lack skills and a work ethic.

Ghetto criminals don't want to hear that crime is bad for victims because they do not identify with their crime victims. They don't want to hear about victim rights because they don't wish anybody opposing their means of self-support. Black racist criminals thus see crime as a career and see potential White crime victims as cannon fodder for their lifestyle.

Envy is common among thieves. If a thief sees something he wants, he becomes envious. He initiates criminal violence against his victim to relieve his emotional resentment by stealing and taking possession of what the other person owns. When Black thieves see what suburban White men have, they become envious because they do not have it, and go on to steal it because they want it, like a hungry wolf spotting a small animal and snatching it for dinner.

Ghetto culture allows career criminals to get away from crime, but their victims are not so lucky. Black racist criminals never respect crime victims. White victims thus should never respect those who perpetrate crimes against Whites or discriminate against Whites.

Sometimes blacks help Whites escape attacks initiated by groups of Blacks, and such Samaritans almost always either come from outside the ghetto or are foreign-born blacks who do not subscribe to the premises of ghetto culture.

Ghetto Attitudes Towards Crime

Black men often tell Black women that they believe that "there are too many Black men in prison already." That is a form of Black-on-Black behavioral expectation used to socially pressure Black women not to file criminal charges against Black men who attack them. Note that this situation involves Black-on-Black crime, with no Whites involved. Those who not conform to the cultural ideals of the ghetto made to feel socially unwelcome in the ghetto.

Those espousing such opinions do not mention that too many people have been made into crime victims by Black men. If there one Black criminal who is not in prison for his crimes, then there are not enough Black men in jail. Criminals and those who identify with them routinely intimidate and mislead crime victims and witnesses, and this is one way in which they do it. Black racists do similar things to Whites as part of their standard operating procedure for dealing with actual and potential victims and witnesses. Fraud and misrepresentation are tools they use to control other people's thoughts and actions.

The same principle applies to Whites, Asians, and Blacks, who act "White." Anyone who is not "Black" by the standards of definition espoused by Black ghetto racists, almost all of whom are career criminals, are regarded as outsiders. Black racists feel entitled to commit crimes against because they are "not one of us." Ghetto culture glorifies criminals, including Black racist criminals, and marginalizes outsiders, crime victims in general, and Whites in particular.

Black Racism In The Media

The mass media occasionally carry news stories that include video recordings of Blacks, often in gangs or smaller wolf-pack groups, attacking a lone White in public places such as restaurants. Black racists do this because they think that the lone White individual wore unusual clothing, or was guilty of being White, or some other sort of everyday behavior that the Blacks in question saw as an excuse for violence. That is a ghetto overseer mentality.

Ghetto culture legitimizes random violence against Whites at the personal discretion of Black racist criminals. It marginalizes their victims for bogus reasons such a White's clothing, speech, or other aspects of their behavior. Black criminals often say words to the effect that White crime victims "had it coming" or that the attackers "didn't mean it" (a standard characterization of Black-on-White criminal behavior) or "that's the way Black people are, don't get in their way."

Blacks racist usually believe that they are "entitled" to commit crimes against Whites without fear of punishment. They are the products of a lower-class ghetto culture where violence is the norm, and violent criminals idolized. Ghetto culture hates and envies Whites, so ghetto culture says that anything goes where Whites are involved.

One common symptom of everyday Black Racism is Black beggars asking White strangers on the street, to "loan" them money. Ghetto culture legitimizes lying to Whites and defrauding them of money. Such beggars should apply for loans from their parole officers. If they don't have one as yet, they will have one eventually.

Black-initiated violence against Whites for no real reason is not a topic that Black racists talk into it. Their disregard for the interests of White crime victims reflects their Black racist overseer mentality. Violence is the norm when Blacks feel like doing it to Whites. However, White self-defense and the criminal prosecution of Black criminals are taboo subjects for Black racists.

White victims of Black racist crimes are quite aware that some Blacks routinely pretend not to see Black-On-White crimes that go on right in front of them. Blacks of the pro-criminal mentality never cooperate with the legal system to punish Blacks for sins and don't care about the White victims of such crimes, because they see no need to respect Whites in any way. Blacks who don't report crimes do so because they see criminal activities like the standard way of life in the ghetto where many Blacks believe they are entitled to commit crimes.

Many Blacks see no evil, hear no evil, and speak no evil regarding Black-on-White crimes. It applied to theft and bullying in schools, fraudulent charges of racism on the job, and street crime. Their viewpoint is that whatever happens to a White person that is perpetrated by a Black racist is something that they couldn't care less. The only time that they care is when a Black criminal caught, at which point they charge the White crime victim with being a racist.

Chapter 9: How to end racism?

Racism is the point at which somebody is dealt with contrastingly on account of their race or culture. It can incorporate things like calling individuals names or barring them and in any event, denying them administration at a business or something like openings for work. It's unlawful in the UK to victimize (treat quickly) somebody on account of their race. If you or somebody you know is encountering racism, you can find support to make this stop.

Try not to take the maltreatment.

Everybody, regardless of what their nationality or race is, has an option to live joyfully and liberated from separation. On the off chance that you feel somebody's bigot towards you, Child line has data about what steps you can take. The primary concern is to leave, be careful and converse with somebody you trust. You don't have to fight back or react.

If you feel you've been oppressed unlawfully, for instance, grinding away or by a business, you can discover your privileges at Citizens Advice. If somebody is supremacist towards you, the most significant thing is your wellbeing. On the off chance that you feel helpless, stay with gatherings of companions you trust, on the chance that you or somebody you know is in quick or dangerous peril, dial 999. Keep in mind; you're not the one raising a ruckus. You've done nothing incorrectly.

Keep proof
Keep a journal of what's been occurring and spare any writings or messages to show others how it is influencing you and what bolster you need. If you make a move, any proof you can assemble will support your case.

Tell somebody
Address your instructors, youth laborers, companions as well as a family about what's happening with the goal that you can get their assistance and backing. In case you don't know how to begin the discussion, Childline has valuable data about how to approach a grown-up for help.

Report it
You can report supremacist occurrences to Police Scotland by visiting your neighborhood police headquarters, rounding out an online structure. Resident's Advice Scotland has more data about what happens when you report an occurrence, what data you'll be requested and what may occur after the

episode has been accounted for. At the point when you say the event, you ought to seek the episode reference number. On the off chance that you experience issues talking or getting English, you can request that the police give a translator - they should provide you with one.

Keep in mind: you don't need to be the race or culture that somebody has expected you are the point at which they state or plan something for you with the goal for it to be a detest wrongdoing or occurrence. Discover progressively about hate wrongdoing and episodes and how to report them.

Remain safe on the web
In case you're encountering misuse on the web, you can generally report it utilizing the 'report misuse' button on most online networking stages. Ensure your protection settings are secure, as well. The UK Safer Internet Center has a few assets remembering guides for how to ensure every one of your web-based life accounts is private and secure.

You can likewise distinct square individuals on the off chance that they're irritating or harassing you. We have a guide on the best way to square individuals on each internet-based life stage. The foundation Glitch has a valuable asset to assist you with recording any online maltreatment which can be utilized as proof if you later make a report to the police.

Get others included
Only discussing racism is a significant piece of battling it. You could begin an enemy of racism venture or bulletin at your school/youth gathering or set up a conversation gathering to discuss relevant issues and what you can do to help.

Never surrender!
You probably won't have the option to handle racism without anyone else; however, we would all be able to have an impact. Testing racism when you see it (without putting yourself in danger) and revealing it assists with making others see it's not alright.

Bolster others
On the off chance that you see or hear somebody being supremacist towards another person, you can assist with supporting that individual. Directly inquiring as to whether they're alright and telling them that what you saw wasn't right can genuinely help. You could assist them with reporting it on the off chance that they need and offer to be an observer. This is called Third Party Reporting.

If you feel good and the circumstance implies it's protected to do as such, you can likewise challenge racism when you see it by saying you don't concur with it.

Activity on Prejudice has an asset, called Speak Up, to assist you with seeing how you can be what is called a functioning observer, this implies when somebody sees struggle or unsatisfactory conduct they make strides that can have any kind of effect in a sheltered and fitting manner.

Uprooting racism

Activists talk about how you position yourself against racism and discrimination.

Hundreds of thousands of people in the United States and around the world have been taking to the streets to protest racism, injustice, and police violence in the United States for days.

At the same time, demands for profound structural changes continue to grow - to end mass arrests, reform police services in the US and elsewhere, invest in black communities, and more.

Though the protests were sparked by the murders of George Floyd, Tony McDade, Breonna Taylor, Ahmaud Arbery, and countless others, centuries of violence and systematic oppression have fueled the protests.

The people who demonstrate on the street and protest on social media call for more solidarity. The demand: end racial inequality once and for all. Here are six ideas on how you can get active now.

1. Support justice beyond origin and skin color - every day.

"Racial justice" is the systematic fair treatment of all people regardless of their race, skin color, and origin to create equal opportunities for everyone.

"Every day gives us 1,000 different ways to choose Racial Justice," said Key Jackson, senior director of movement and capacity building at Race Forward, to Global Citizen. "If you are unable to be on the street, there are 1,000 different ways you can help."

Putting yourself on a reminder regularly and blocking time can help you keep up. For example, you can block an hour every day to read studies or deal with the topic differently.

You should also question your personal everyday decisions if you want to stand up for equality: which organizations do I support, who do I donate money to? Do I shop at shops owned by black people?

The black community in the United States is significantly larger than in Germany - but there is also diversity here - African supermarkets, hairdressers, and companies that are operated by People of Color. In the first step, you should open your eyes to it, spot new businesses, and put your foot in the door.

If we do that, we will make another contribution to supporting the black community during this time.

2. Get informed!

Education always plays a crucial role in changing things, says Shakti Butler, chairman and founder of World Trust, an organization fighting for social justice and equality.

"People have to do many things," Butler told Global Citizen. "You have to educate yourself. You have to be willing, to be honest with yourself and not deny the truth. "

Based on this education, they have to team up with other people who do the same thing and then decide: how do we make the world a better place? We have to understand what changes are, how they happen, and we have to work together to initiate changes - even if they are small changes.

Whites have to be aware of their privileges. There are a dozen different ways to approach the issue. Listening to podcasts, reading articles, and studies - it would all help.

3. Donate money

It is also helpful to donate money to organizations that are directed in particular by People of Color and work on the subject of anti-racism. For example, in Germany, you can donate to the Black People Initiative (ISD Bund), Each One Teach One, or Kop Berlin, which campaigned against racial profiling.

In the United States, there is also a big problem with the bail law in many states: "Cash Bail." An offender who is charged can, under certain conditions, avoid pre-trial detention and "buy himself out" until his trial if he leaves a deposit. The judge usually determines the sum. This leads to great social injustice and prefers the rich. California was the first US state to abolish the system in 2018. But in many other states, it is still commonplace.

Therefore, it is worthwhile to donate to so-called "bail funds," which are intended to support those who cannot pay the deposit themselves.

Bail Funds are initiatives that seek to intervene immediately in criminalizing poverty and in the idea that people can only be free if they have the money to get out of poverty.

The Bail Project created a national emergency hotline for rescue operations that anyone can call to rescue a friend or family member.

You can also donate directly to families of people who have been killed by the police. The families of George Floyd, Tony McDade, Ahmaud Arbery, and countless other people murdered by the police need financial support to pay legal bills.

4. Have difficult conversations.

Perhaps one of the most important tips: talk to each other, conduct complex discussions and debates. Amnesty International recommends that people name racism when they see it - and condemn it.

This moment allows us to have conversations that we have never had before, to go deeper and be ready to push, push, and be pushed ourselves.

Talk to your friends, acquaintances, neighbors, fellow students, and professors and read and comment on social media!

5. Go vote and become politically active!

No matter whether in local elections, Bundestag elections, or European elections: Every vote counts! Voting is so crucial for political participation and participation. With elections, we can ensure that injustice is addressed and alleviated.

But there are also many ways to become politically active beyond elections. You can join a party or become active online by signing petitions, sending emails to MPs, or sending tweets asking politicians to act. This is exactly what you can do with Global Citizen. On our platform, you will find actions on topics related to the United Nations' sustainable development goals to end extreme poverty by 2030 and ensure a fairer world.

The Color of Change organization also recommends signing the #JusticeForFloyd petition to be held accountable to the officers responsible for the death of George Floyd.

6. Demonstrate!

Demonstrations have always been a powerful tool to fight for human rights. Regardless of whether against right-wing violence against police violence in the USA or apartheid in South Africa: demonstrations have played an important role in the history of human rights movements but also the recent past.

Of course, it is more difficult than usual during the current pandemic and the restrictions on the meeting. So please pay attention to the contact and meeting regulations in your (federal) country and to wear a mask where necessary.

And last but not least: make a statement, show solidarity - now immediately!

We do not doubt that some white people are as disgusted with the system as we are. But it does not make sense to speak of a coalition if there is no one to ally with because of the lack of white organization. (…) The question is whether the whites will have the courage to invest in white neighborhoods to organize them. (…) How are they going to mobilize people around a concept of whiteness based on real brotherhood and aimed at putting an end to economic exploitation, so that black people have a group with which to ally themselves? If a coalition is needed to bring about real social change in this country, white people must start building such organizations in their community. This is the pressing question facing white activists today.

Create a white anti-racist community

For many, this seems contradictory: "Isn't it racist to be only between white people? Is this not another form of segregation? These are the reasons why it seems important to us to create a white anti-racist community:

- Non-color people should not be the only ones educating white people about racism and their oppression.

- To overcome racism and challenge white supremacy, white people must unlearn racism and discover how we reproduce white privilege. It is a long, difficult, and sometimes painful path.

- The commitment to build an anti-racist identity and practice as a white person often involves conflict in our lives, especially with our friends and family members who disagree with us. AWARE is a space where you can get the support of other people who face the same difficulties as white anti-racists.

- It is a space where white people can find out what it means to be a white anti-racist and to question racism in all spheres of their lives.

- It's a place where whites can learn to build a new anti-racism culture and learn the skills to transform white society.

- AWARE complements but does not replace activist spaces and interracial dialogues between whites and people of color.

An old militant tradition which knows a new vigor

White anti-racist movements were not born with BLM and the election of Donald Trump. If movements mark the history of the anti-slavery and anti-segregationist struggle, the question arises vigorously with the emergence of the civil rights movement when one of its flagship organizations, the SNCC, decides to exclude the whites so that the first concerned, the blacks lead the fight. This exclusion results in the creation of some white anti-racist and anti-imperialist organizations, which declined in the early 1970s. It was not until several decades later, in the wake of the protests against the WTO in Seattle and the birth of the anti-globalization movement, which this question resurfaced in the United States. Certain activists of color criticize in particular paternalistic practices or even the blindness to the racial stakes associated with the fight against the neo-liberalism of the white militants. This is how groups begin to form locally, like Catalyst in San Francisco or AWARE in Los Angeles, created in 2003.

Deconstructing white privilege through speech

AWARE is made up of two main branches: "Saturday dialogues" and "White People for Black Lives" (WP4BL). Organized once a month, the dialogues on Saturday consist of discussion groups focusing for example on "the last time your privilege as a white man struck you," "difficulties in being a white anti-racist," "what allows us as a white man not to have to ask the question of our racial identity "or" how racism serves to divide the working class and allow the reproduction of capitalism, "to hang only a few examples to which I have been able to assist. The challenge is to deconstruct racism internalized by collective discussion. Recalling feminist advocacy groups, AWARE wants to be more of a "brave space" than a "safe space," as Dahlia, one of the organizers put it: "because as white people we are used to putting our comfort first, but here we want to take risks. The risks in question are mostly personal, in the ability of individuals to engage, to share their stories, their suffering, and their doubts, and to challenge their prejudices to uproot the white supremacy that structures American society. The meetings are nonetheless very inclusive and can only strike by the quality of the listening, the respect, and the delicacy shown by the participants towards their interlocutors.

At the start of each session, we take turns reading the "communication rules for a brave space," which underline in nine points and in a very deliberative way the importance of listening, not to take up too much space and accept the disagreement. One of the rules also invites us to "use this space to recognize and investigate our privileges (for example class, gender, sexual orientation, validity) and to honor the different experiences that we each bring with us in this space. As is often the case with far-left militant groups in the United States, the first round also invites everyone to state their name, but also their "preferred gender pronoun," "he, she or they," the group taking into account the constructed character of gender identities and the desire to overcome traditional binary oppositions. This strong reflexivity as to the intersectionality of the forms of domination is perhaps reinforced by the sociology of the participants, very majority of middle and higher class: the majority have a university degree and a job, the intellectual and artistic professions. Are overrepresented, as are young people aged 25 to 40. Note that some groups - elsewhere in the United States - have set up subgroups for the working classes, temporary unmixedness can also have virtues to fight class domination.

Control strategies

The other branch of AWARE, White People for Black Lives, aims to organize direct actions independently or connected with the movements of people of color. The organization thus takes part in the weekly Black Lives Matter demonstrations against the "Los Angeles police commission," like any other direct action organized by BLM. Thus, in the summer of 2016, when BLM "occupied" the town hall of Los Angeles - holding a camp for more than a month - the white allies played an important role, both in providing logistical aid to the camp and in intervening between black activists and the police when violence was near. Solidarity also requires financial support, AWARE raising funds - several tens of thousands of dollars in three years in Los Angeles - to pay for any legal fees or logistical costs associated with BLM's mobilizations. However, this support rarely comes through public speaking by white activists, who remain in the background of the mobilizations. During presentation speaking turns at BLM monthly meetings, white people present themselves - when they have integrated the discursive norms that regulate this space - as seeking to "learn to become a better ally" or "to help the movement, according to the methods that you think are the most relevant. AWARE has theorized these forms of collaboration as part of a "transformative alliance" model. It is a question for the white anti-racist movements of working on solidarity with the struggles of racialized people and, at the same time, working on the deconstruction of the white privilege within the white community.

WP4BL thus organizes its demonstrations to challenge the white population before their inaction in the face of racism. These are symbolic actions that show solidarity with the struggles of racialized people and demonstrate that the fight against racism does not only concern its victims. By calling on white people, these direct actions also aim to encourage action by previously passive sympathizers. These tactics are part of the organization's theory of social change.

AWARE has been a member since 2007 of a national white anti-racist organization, Showing Up for Racial Justice (SURJ), which defends the theory of "closest hanging fruit." The objective of the organization is to grow and convince more and more white people of the need to fight systemic racism, and this work of conviction can only be done step by step. Rather than trying to convince people who are very socially distant - probably more difficult to influence - it is better first to target sympathizers, relatives, sensitive to the theme but previously inactive. It is, therefore, by working on oneself and convincing those close to you that social change, from below, will be possible. If the way to widen the circle is not methodically theorized, AWARE nevertheless organizes actions aimed at reaching more people. Thus, every weekend, activists go to markets in neighborhoods that are deemed to be predominantly white and progressive (and therefore also often upper-middle class), hold a stand, publicize the organization, have conversations with the interested people and possibly convince them to participate in a first meeting.

The election of Donald Trump as President of the United States nevertheless strongly affected the organization, both locally and nationally. Not only has the number of participants in monthly meetings tripled, but new methods have also been developed. Convinced that the Trump election was due in part to the vote of the white population (and not that the "white working class" frequently pointed out) and embodied a form of racial resentment, some member organizations of SURJ have decided to embark on the practice of "deep canvassing" or "deep door-to-door

To chat with and possibly convince Trump voters. It seemed true to some that the nearest fruit's theory would never be sufficient to reach the voters most socially distant from the militants. If the Los Angeles branch has not, to date, embarked on such practices, that of New York, where I participated in the spring of 2017, has been carrying out intensive plowing work since January.

They then choose a neighborhood that has mostly voted for Trump (there are some, including New York), and mostly white, and spend several hours knocking on doors to enter into conversation with the locals. If most decline the invitation, discussions sometimes start. However, that "deep" conversations of a few tens of minutes on their electoral choice or their relationship to the violence suffered by blacks are sufficient to change opinions, sometimes deeply rooted. But experimental studies have already shown, on other subjects, which the method was bearing fruit, and that one in ten conversations resulted in conversion. Thus, in the eyes of these activists, a few tens of thousands of door-to-door discussions could have prevented Donald Trump from winning key states (where the result was very close) and, therefore, the election…

A necessary reflection

The purpose of this chapter is not so much to argue for the identical reproduction of these American experiences in the context but to contribute to a reflection which has difficulty in structuring concerning the place of the whites. In or alongside anti-racist movements.

If most of the anti-racism actors agree that it is legitimate for the first concerned by these questions to lead the struggles, what place is left for the whites? For some, defending a form of radical autonomy, none, it is not the problem of white people, and we are better off without them. For others, a majority, the place of the whites is that of allies. Like BLM's white allies in the United States, the struggles must be waged by those primarily concerned but supported (behind the processions, logistically, symbolically, etc.) by organizations or groups that do not count, not mainly the first concerned. These mobilizations aim in particular to influence laws and public policies by the balance of power and the number; all goodwill, therefore, seems welcome. If, as American activists advance, the overcoming of racism is a condition for the liberation of the whites themselves, can we not envisage a more active role?

Racism is being largely issued and legitimized by the elites. An important field of struggle is the battle of ideas and the deconstruction of racism from above, which legitimizes "toothless racism." If racism is structural and institutional, one of the challenges is to attack its symbolic and ideological roots through a struggle for hegemony. This fight is also here firstly led by the first concerned, the Party of the Indigenous of the Republic, like other militant groups ensuring this political work for several years. They sometimes associate with a certain number of white intellectuals, who appear as so many traveling companions.

One can nevertheless wonder whether it would not be desirable to go beyond the highly individualized nature of these speeches to structure them more collectively. Last summer, white intellectuals, and activists took a stand to defend spaces of temporary unmixedness. Beyond that, one of the central issues in the struggle for hegemony concerns white privilege. However, very little work or intellectual mobilization has been devoted to this question, which nevertheless constitutes the logical counterpart of racist discrimination. Now we can think that putting this issue in the public arena would probably have more weight if it was not only for racialized people but also for the first concern, the whites.

Finally, if racism is systemic and elite, that does not mean that we should not seek to build mass organizations to challenge it. The risk of systemic analysis is indeed to let think that intellectual mobilizations from above could be sufficient. Social change often occurs at the confluence of mass movements and struggles for ideological hegemony. If, once again, the first concerned must be on the front line, can we completely do without white people, including those who are a priori the most distant from these issues?

It seems to me that the United States, political work is to be carried out with white, politically disaffiliated people whose social suffering sometimes takes the form of racist anger. For this work to have a chance of bearing fruit, it is necessary to start from the anger, the problems expressed by people, and then virtualize and deconstruct them. However, this work can only leave traces in the long term if it also takes up the racial question, rather than dodging it as many progressive organizations do, which prefer to put a modest veil on these questions. However, the rise of the National Front indicates that the avoidance of discrimination by a large part of the left has not prevented the progression of racist ideas in recent decades. It is not enough to speak of class - ignoring racial domination - to contribute to the unification of the popular classes. This strategy has always led to the marginalization of minority groups and the racial challenges of "progressive" mobilizations.

Therefore, the path is narrow between anti-racist movements, which either speak in the place of the first concerned or dodge class issues and left movements that refuse to recognize the intersectionality of forms of domination. It is not said, however, that history is doomed to repeat itself. The convergences which are built today around political anti-racism, in particular on the question of police violence, indicate forms of the coalition which, if not mass movements bring together fractions of the extreme who have long ignored each other.

There are probably no simple solutions to these questions, and it is only through experimentation and trial and error that progress will be possible. White people must nevertheless play a more active role in the fight against racist discrimination that plagues society without taking the place of the first concern, as has often been the case in the past. The first issue in the struggle is to recall the virtues that the non-mixed spaces chosen and temporary may have represented in the history of social movements in the emancipation of subordinate groups. Republican ideology and its fear of communities and "communitarianism" has come to make people forget that the inter-self, the hidden spaces, constitute an essential weapon of the dominated, even if they must remain temporary.

Chapter 10: The Importance of Achieving Your Dreams

The art of achieving self-love lies in making yourself happy. Have you set any dreams or goals in childhood or anytime in the past? Have you ever dreamed about becoming a pilot, a doctor, a nurse, an engineer, a footballer, writing a book, or traveling to Thailand? Well, if you want to love yourself, then you need to focus on you and your dreams. All of those dreams that you disregarded or you labeled them, 'Forgotten' or 'Unachievable'

Nothing in this world is impossible it just depends upon how badly you wish for it. If you want something, you'll work hard for it and the chances are you can achieve it. When you want something; all the universe conspires in helping you to achieve it you just have to put the work in.

When we achieve our goals it gives us a sense of achievement and that is a great tool in developing self-esteem. It means we understand that we don't have to necessarily rely on others and it opens the floodgates to what is truly possible.

Seek Success without defining yourself by failure

Some people find it difficult to indulge in self-love because they define themselves by failures rather than their successes. There isn't any substitute for self-love. Some people work a lot and become successful in achieving plenty of success but they still fail when it comes to self-love. These kinds of people are known as overachievers or workaholics. A workaholic is a person who works compulsively. While the term generally implies that the person enjoys their work, it can also alternately imply that they simply feel compelled to do it. These kinds of people often surround themselves with a heavy work load in to disguise their true feelings that they may have about themselves and their lives. We mustn't use success to mask our inner World in such a way that it becomes just another firefighter for our subconscious wounds. The sad thing about it is that there is just a masking process going on, they have developed in one area of life but forgotten the most important.

There is an excess of such people who earn far less than overachievers and workaholics, but they look happier because they fall in love with themselves. Unfortunately, it's just due to a negative philosophy of western society.

People who love themselves always emit rays of positivity while people who lack self-love almost always see the negative aspect of life. One of the biggest differences between optimistic people and pessimists' people is what they decide to focus on. So, always choose to see the positive perspectives of your life when possible.

Facts about Confident People

Confident people may come off as cool, calm, and collected in the face of stressful situations but they are human like you are, they just know how to mask their emotions to maintain their composure.

Confident people, although they may appear calm and collected, also suffer from anxiety, and nervousness and also experience that awkward feeling we all dread. They are human and they do feel those nervous flutters, they have just mastered the art of keeping it inwardly focused. It doesn't matter how confident you are, nervousness in front of a crowd is normal and that feeling never goes away. Learn to deal with it as you become more confident and keep that cool and calm exterior.

Confident people are more easily able to manage their emotions. Yes, the feel the emotions they have just learned how to control what is shown on the outside, only allowing emotions that are appropriate for that moment, escape. Managing your emotions takes time and practice and you have to learn to set the right mindset to deal with the situation. Your emotions should not be allowed to guide your actions. You have the power to control the situation.

People who display huge confidence are often those who have performed or spoken in front of large audiences for a very long time. They admit to feeling the nerves beforehand but once on stage their instinct to perform takes over. Their skills have been acquired through routine and repetitiveness.

Confident people are not afraid to let people see their weaknesses or their vulnerability. They take risks even when failure is a possibility. They don't allow failure to define who they are. They are open and willing to take criticism and learn and grow from it but at the same time, they don't define themselves by what others think of them. They know their worth and that is why they have that wonderful feeling of confidence and security. Know your worth and your life will be full of pleasure and the failures won't be as hard to handle.

That actor who seems so calm in any role or the teacher who seems so at ease speaking to halls full of students, they feel the same fears as you do, they simply know how to manage that fear and the emotions that go along with it and present an exterior that is calm and confident. Lessons that are learned through time and practice. Take your time, nothing worth possessing is easy to obtain or hold on to. Persevere and you will reap the benefits of your hard work sooner than you may think.

Conclusion

Every human being, despite their race or nationality, deserves to live a happy, peaceful life, free of discrimination in any form. Racism has been sown so deeply into the subconscious of Americans. It might seem overwhelming to deal with, but as an anti-racist, you need to choose social justice every day.

It is my deepest, sincerest hope that you are filled with motivation and inspiration to begin your journey towards anti-racism at the end of this book. You have grown much more than you realize in your understanding of race and racial bias by choosing to read through this to the very end with an open mind. You may not know it yet, but you are not only developing into a better version of yourself, you are also cultivating a clearer picture of racial justice and how to identify it in your daily life. You are helping to craft a better future by teaching your young ones to be loving, accepting, open, and nonjudgment

al to others.

Make it a point of duty to share the steps on racial identity development with others in your community who are open to developing an anti-racist mentality. With increased awareness and knowledge, the destruction of racism and the rebirth of a new society based on justice and acceptance is a dream that is sure to be real in due time.

It is one thing to develop your racial identity as a strategy towards racial healing, but another thing entirely to actively fight for the racially accepting world that we all want and deserve with all that is in you. It will feel exhausting on some days. It will feel like you are being unheard and misunderstood. It will feel like you're continuously running up a brick wall. True.

But don't stop fighting. Because sooner or later, whether now, or generations after, the all-inclusive, all accepting dream will no longer be a dream. It will be very, very real.

And it will be because you kept up the good fight.

© Courtney Fernandez

Made in the USA
Monee, IL
19 October 2020